GLASGOW'S
GAELIC CHURCHES

GLASGOW'S GAELIC CHURCHES

Highland religion
in an urban setting
1690-1995

Ian R MacDonald

The Knox Press (Edinburgh)

THE KNOX PRESS (EDINBURGH)
15 North Bank Street, Edinburgh EH1 2LS

© I R MacDonald 1995
First published 1995

ISBN 0 904422 66 6

Art work by Donald M Shearer
Typeset by HEBS Inverness
Printed by Highland Printers, Inverness

Publication assisted by a grant from the Catherine McCaig Trust

FOREWORD

L ike many Highlanders, I have had a long association, through several generations, with Glasgow's Gaelic churches. I am proud of that association and count it an honour to introduce this excellent account of their history.

These churches had an enormous spiritual impact on Highland migrants to Glasgow. Dislocated and confused, the new arrivals found welcome and reassurance in congregations which spoke a familiar language and reflected familiar values. With few exceptions the pulpits of these churches preached biblical Christianity; and did so with clarity and passion. It was such preaching as changed lives, particularly those of the young. Many were challenged by the lordship of Christ and moved beyond second-hand allegiance to an intelligent personal commitment to Christianity.

The Glasgow Gaelic churches were also remarkable in their sociology. They drew their membership from the working classes: men from the shipyards, the dredgers and the granary; women from domestic service and the factory floor. During the week these immigrants toiled for long hours and low wages. But on Sunday they were aristocrats, dressed in their finest and rising to the full height of human dignity in intelligent, enraptured worship of their Maker. On such days, I suspect, they felt superior to their masters; who, although they might have been giants in the world of commerce, were dwarfs in the world of the spirit. Any employer who visited these Gaelic services (and some did) would have been viewed with the compassion appropriate to the backward.

Dr MacDonald's narrative brings out, too, the full extent of the denominational divisions and internal disputes which disfigure this history. But it also indicates the fluidity of denominational barriers in Gaelic Scotland. The lure of the language and its distinctive liturgy triumphed over all else. Nor was this confined to the remote past. The former minister of one of the Church of Scotland's Gaelic congregations told me recently that they discontinued their Friday Fellowship Meetings only when the generation of Free Church speakers on whose support they relied passed away. The divisions of Presbyterianism are often seen at their most offensive in small Highland communities. But they seldom originated there. The Gaelic churches were victims of denominationalism, not its perpetrators.

Glasgow's Gaelic churches faced a constant struggle to keep up their numerical strength. Every year, large numbers of those who had come to the end of their working lives left the city to spend their retirement "at home" (a reminder that the flow of spiritual capital was not all in one direction). Besides, it was always difficult to retain second-generation immigrants. The original exiles loved the Gaelic ethos of their churches and derived solace and security from it. For their children, it was different. Their knowledge of Gaelic was limited; their friends went elsewhere; and when they married, their spouses found the ambience of the Gaelic churches alien and threatening.

This problem faces immigrant churches in all cultures. How can one be simultaneously loyal to the old and relevant to the new? It was tempting to say, "There are plenty English-speaking churches. Let them go there!" But this would have meant parents going to one church and children to another. The only feasible approach, apart from trying to reinstate Gaelic as the national language of Scotland, would have been to introduce bilingualism.

This was done, eventually. But *eventually* was too late. By that time the flow of Highland migrants had dried up, and the Gaelic churches were showing symptoms of a new disease: upward social mobility. The Gael had long had a passion for education and the city gave abundant opportunity to indulge it. The children of Gaelic labourers became teachers, doctors and accountants, moved from Partick to Bearsden and fitted less and less easily into the churches of their roots.

By the 1980s a new dawn had broken. Gaelic had acquired respectability and Evangelicalism had become middle-class. Again it was too late. The historic Highland churches now provided only token Gaelic services.

Today, we are living in the midst of a Gaelic renaissance, but the churches have been slow to capitalise on it. One can only express the hope that Christianity will not turn its back on the products of Gaelic-medium education, the producers of Gaelic television and the small army of poets, musicians and dramatists who have been so successful in dragging Gaelic culture into the European mainstream.

Such are the issues that come under scrutiny in this book. The author, Dr Ian MacDonald, belongs to a rare breed: a research scientist with a passion for history, a love of literature and a hunger for theology.

This book reflects these qualities. Dr MacDonald has chosen a neglected subject and researched it as meticulously as, in another capacity, he investigated the effect of environmental forces on plant growth. He provides the reader with a mass of fascinating information, concluding with two chapters of thoughtful (and thought-provoking) reflection. The whole is presented with lucidity and elegance. It whets the appetite for more. In the meantime, I am delighted to see this story in print.

Donald Macleod
Free Church College
April, 1995.

ACKNOWLEDGEMENTS

I have been the recipient of many kindnesses in this attempt to summon up the past and bring to light from a neglected and forgotten literature aspects of a religious life now almost beyond recall. The staff of the Scottish Record Office, Edinburgh, afforded me every possible assistance in surroundings highly conducive to prolonged and digressive research. The staff of the Mitchell Library, Glasgow, were no less helpful and considerate. In respect of archival material I am particularly indebted to the Rev. Ronald G. Mackay, former minister of St Vincent St. Free Church and his Kirk Session for permission to borrow and scrutinize at leisure all the extant records of Hope St. Gaelic Church. I am similarly obligated to the Rev. Donald N. Macleod, minister of Grant St. Free Church, Glasgow, and his Kirk Session for like access to the records of Duke St. Free Gaelic Church.

Many other ministers of the Free Church of Scotland have contributed to my awareness of times past, not least among them the late Rev. Hugh G. Mackay, minister in Aberdeen from 1948 - 1965, who himself grew up in an environment of Highland piety at its most impressive flowering. Happily, many from whom I have benefited over the years remain to this present time, among them Professor Donald Macleod whose theological and homilectical gifts place him alongside the most notable preachers that people these pages. I am much indebted to him for honouring me by contributing a preface. Many will discern the signs of his perceptive thinking not just in the foreword but no less obviously in the sequel.

I am grateful also to those who have encouraged me and helped me to bring the fruit of my research to the notice of a wider public. The Rev. John J Murray, secretary of the Knox Press, Edinburgh, enlisted his publishing know-how to my advantage. The enthusiasm of Donald W Macleod, former rector of Fortrose Academy, for harnessing new technology to serve the needs of daily life, has impressed me for half a century and now his practical skills in the labyrinthine ways of desktop publishing proved to be a major encouragement in the present enterprise. Donald M Shearer, another good friend of long standing, on learning of my fruitless archival search for a cover photograph, met my need with his delightful artistry.

Finally my thanks to home and family for maintaining an environment that indulged my fondness for contemplating

"the times and ages that are past

full many years agone".

Ian R. MacDonald
Cults, Aberdeen.

CONTENTS

INTRODUCTION

For centuries the history of Glasgow was the history of its ecclesiastical community. Then came the industrial revolution and the consequent growth and development of Glasgow's manufacturing and commercial life gave historians new materials with which to chronicle its prosperity. In comparison with its rising trade and industry, Glasgow's ecclesiastical history now seemed of little consequence. Even so, religion continued to play a significant role in the life of the community. "Let Glasgow flourish by the preaching of the Word" was the city's motto until recent times. However, despite the close involvement of religion with Glasgow's nineteenth century life, much of the church history of that period has still to be written. What follows is an attempt to outline the rise and dissolution of Glasgow's Gaelic churches.

Although Gaelic preachers occupied the Tron and Ramshorn pulpits from the late seventeenth century, it was not until 1770 that the first chapel to be specifically dedicated to Gaelic preaching was erected on Ingram St. In due course additional chapels appeared on Duke St. (1798), Hope St. (1824), Oswald St. (1847), Maitland St. (1861) and other places. As these congregations grew and prospered the original chapels were replaced with later structures. Now all of them early and late alike, have disappeared without trace. Church extension has given way to church extinction. Impressive monuments to Glasgow's once burgeoning church life have been obliterated. The city's ecclesiastical heritage, especially its nineteenth century heritage, has suffered grievously at the hands of planners and improvers. The visible history of the Gaelic church has perished.

Today the annalist of Glasgow's Highland church life is dependent on archival deposits but here too there are disappointments. Firstly, the early buildings predated photography and later ones found no favour with Glasgow's acclaimed photographers. Secondly, church records are notoriously vulnerable to destruction. Session clerks, or management committee clerks, are often less than punctilious with respect to collating and safeguarding documents. Earlier records are not always transferred with the clerkship. The newly appointed clerk is concerned only with the minute book in current use. Of earlier records he may have no awareness and, unknown and unsought, the sundered records are left behind, eventually to be discarded by the indifferent heirs of his predecessor. Fortunately for our purposes some records, although far from complete, have survived for almost all of the major centres of Gaelic preaching. It is from these fragmented records written entirely in English, as was the common practice in all Gaelic churches, whether Lowland or Highland, that the story unfolds.

1   GLASGOW'S HIGHLANDERS AND THE CHURCH'S MISSION

D ating the formation of permanent colonies of Gaelic-speaking Highlanders in most Lowland towns is largely a matter of guesswork and Glasgow is no exception. A recognisable Highland community became established in the city in the late seventeenth century and possibly earlier. The size of the Gaelic community in the decades prior to the 1881 census (the first official recording of Gaelic speakers) has been variously estimated. In 1722, in the pleadings relative to the translation of the Rev. John MacLaurin from Luss to Glasgow, it was argued that there were "more in Glasgow who do not understand the language spoken in the Lowlands than at Luss".[1] At that time the population of Luss numbered about one thousand but Gaelic speakers were in a minority and Glasgow's Gaelic community may not have exceeded that figure.

When a petition for permission to open a second Gaelic Chapel was presented in 1798, it was claimed that there had been a very great influx of Highlanders into the city and suburbs for years past, "not near one half of whom can be accommodated in the present Gaelic Chapel".[2] That chapel had 1090 sittings. Given that many Highlanders would not want to purchase a chapel sitting, it would seem that by the end of the eighteenth century there were several thousand Highlanders in Glasgow's 70,000 population. In the early nineteenth century the number continued to grow exponentially. In 1824 a petition for the establishment of another Gaelic chapel affirmed that "at a moderate computation the number of inhabitants in Glasgow and the suburbs who were born in the Highlands is not less than 30,000".[3] According to James Cleland, who was appealed to for accurate information, Glasgow's population

---

1   SRO, CH. 1/2/46, Assembly papers, f.253-277: Transportation of John MacLaurin from Luss to Glasgow, 10 July 1722. Reasons from commissioners from Glasgow.
2   SRO, CH. 2/171/15, Minutes of the Presbytery of Glasgow, 28 March 1798, p. 158.
3   SRO, CH. 16/3/1/1, Minutes of Managers' meeting, Hope St. Gaelic Chapel March 1823.

at that time was 150,000 but he was reluctant to put a figure on the Highland community saying, "I am sorry that it is not in my power to give you the necessary information respecting the number of Highlanders in this city and suburbs with any degree of accuracy". He had, at one time, been anxious himself to ascertain the number of Highlanders "but was obliged to give up the idea from the difficulty of finding out who could and could not receive instruction in the English language".[4] Ten years later that problem may have been resolved when the three existing Gaelic churches together undertook, in 1835, a systematic survey of all Gaelic speakers in Glasgow. That census revealed that there were 20,000 persons above ten years of age capable of receiving instruction only in Gaelic.[5] (Incidentally that survey was undertaken with a view to allocating parish territory to each congregation in accordance with the provisions of the Chapel Act of 1834. Although the Presbytery drew up provisional boundaries, these were never implemented because of the failure of the Gaelic ministers to agree, Norman Macleod of St Columba's maintaining the historic position that his parish was the City of Glasgow.) The influx of Highlanders continued unabated and by the middle of the nineteenth century the Free Church Highland Committee estimated Glasgow's Gaelic community as 45,000.[6] If the absolute figure was not to rise much above this level thereafter, the proportion of Gaelic speakers residing in the Lowlands relative to those in the Gaidhealtachd, continued on its upward course until eventually there were more Gaelic speakers in Strathclyde than in the Western Isles.[7]

4   SRO, CH. 16/3/1/1, Letter from Mr Cleland to Mr McGeorge dated 24 Dec. 1823.
5   J. N. Macleod, *Memorials of the Rev. Norman Macleod, D.D.*(Edinburgh, 1898), p. 115.
6   Report of the Highland Committee to the General Assembly 1855. Proceedings of the Free Church of Scotland General Assembly 1855, p. 23.
7   D.S. Thomson, (ed.), *The Companion to Gaelic Scotland* (Oxford, 1983).

The Church's thinking on the need for Gaelic services in Lowland towns was expressed in two quite distinct phases. In the eighteenth century its concern was to supply Gospel ordinances in Gaelic to those who could not understand English sufficiently well to benefit from English language services. In all, seven Gaelic chapels, only one of which was in Glasgow, were opened with this purpose in view.[8] The second phase, which took account of the changing circumstances, occurred in the latter half of the nineteenth century when the Church's mission strategy was directed not so much at monolingual Highlanders, of whom the number was steadily declining, but at bilingual Highlanders whose preference for Gaelic services was regarded as offering a more hopeful avenue for evangelizing the lapsed and the careless. Almost all of the congregations so formed were in Glasgow but many of them were scarcely to rise above the status of mission halls. In between these two territorial campaigns by the Church authorities, other Gaelic congregations were to arise largely as a result of lay initiative. As in the Northern Highlands where zealous evangelical laymen had assumed positions of leadership within the ecclesiastical community, so also among the Highland communities in the cities, laymen took the initiative in forming new congregations. Frequently the incentive for a new start was a disputed ministerial settlement in a vacant congregation. The disaffected minority hived off to form a separate congregation which, before very long, received official recognition by Presbytery. More than one influential congregation of Highlanders was to be formed in this way.

8   For a more detailed account of these chapels see I. R. MacDonald, *The Beginning of Gaelic Preaching in Scotland's Cities*, NORTHERN SCOTLAND, 9, 45-52.

2 GAELIC CHURCHES PRIOR TO 1843

2.1 The Established Church

Although Gaelic preaching in Glasgow was not confined to the Established Church it was very largely identified with it. One of the characteristic features of Highland religion, at least prior to 1843, was the almost total absence of Presbyterian dissent. The failure of the Secession and the Relief Churches to gain a footing in the Highlands has been attributed to their lack of Gaelic-speaking preachers[1] but, making all due allowance for the absence of opportunity, it remains true that Highlanders were not generally attracted to the principles of Dissent.[2] Moreover, in the cities, the need to appoint a Gaelic preacher allowed the Highlanders to circumvent, without recourse to secession, the reluctance of Presbytery to countenance alternative ministries. As a result, Gaelic chapels-of-ease were established with much less opposition than that accorded to their English counterparts.

2.1.1. Gaelic preaching in the Tron and Ramshorn Parish Churches 1690-1754

Before designated Gaelic chapels were erected, Gaelic ministry was dispensed by Gaelic-speaking parish ministers. The Rev. Neil Gillies, inducted to the Tron Kirk in 1690, was a Gaelic preacher noted for "his ministerial skill in that language".[3] His

---

1   J. M'Kerrow, *History of the Secession Church* (Edinburgh, 1845), Revised and enlarged edition, p. 641. G. Struthers, *The History of the Rise, Progress and Principles of the Relief Church* (Glasgow, 1843), p. 400.

2   J. MacInnes, *The Evangelical Movement in the Highlands of Scotland. 1688-1800* (Aberdeen, 1951), p. 90.

3. SR0, CH. 1/2/46, Assembly papers, f. 253-277: Transportation of John MacLaurin from Luss to Glasgow, 10 July 1722. Reasons from commissioners from Glasgow.

practical ministry in Glasgow to sick and dying Highlanders long remained in the memory and his death in 1701 left a void in Gaelic pastoring. It was not until 1717 that any steps were taken to remedy the situation. In that year the Synod of Argyll intervened to fill the gap and an appeal was sent by the Synod to three influential ministers, viz., the Rev. Neil Campbell, Gaelic-speaking minister of Renfrew (and subsequently Principal of Glasgow University), the Rev. Daniel MacLaurin, minister of Rosneath where he had succeeded the aforementioned Neil Campbell, and the Rev. John Anderson, minister of the Northwest Parish (the Ramshorn Kirk) in Glasgow. The Synod's plea to these men was that they would put pressure on the civic authorities to make provision for the spiritual welfare of the Glasgow Highlanders.[4] However, in a matter of months, MacLaurin and Anderson, the men from whom the most sympathetic response might have been expected, were dead; and the Synod, surmising from further correspondence with the Presbytery of Glasgow that "little encouragement is to be expected in this affair at this time", desisted from their efforts.[5] Eventually, an unrelated appointment brought about a satisfactory solution. This was the translation in 1723 of the Rev John MacLaurin, Gaelic-speaking minister at Luss and nephew of the aforementioned Daniel MacLaurin, to succeed the deceased John Anderson in the Ramshorn Kirk. The difficulties which the Synod of Argyll had earlier experienced in their efforts to introduce Gaelic ministry to Glasgow were to reappear when MacLaurin received the call from Glasgow.

4   SRO, CH. 2/557/5, Minutes of the Synod of Argyll, 4 August 1719, p. 238.
5   *Ibid.*, 7 June 1721, p. 268.

The Moderate majority in the Presbytery of Dunbarton refused to loose MacLaurin from the charge of Luss, ostensibly on the grounds that the transference of a Gaelic-speaking minister from a Highland to a Lowland charge was contrary to Assembly legislation enacted in 1694 to prevent the drain of Gaelic ministers from Highland parishes.[6] The actual reason, of course, was a reluctance to translate an evangelical preacher to an influential city pulpit. The Ramshorn congregation appealed to the Commission of Assembly against this refusal pointing out that there were far more Gaelic speakers in Glasgow than in Luss. They also drew attention to the circumstance that concern for the letter of the law re the translation of Gaelic-speaking ministers had not restrained the Presbytery of Dunbarton from agreeing to the translation of the Moderate Gaelic-speaking minister of Rosneath, the Rev Neil Campbell, from the highland parish of Rosneath to the lowland parish of Renfrew.[7] MacLaurin's supporters argued that, in the light of the Presbytery's decision re translating Campbell to Renfrew, justice demanded that MacLaurin should be allowed to go to Glasgow "when the reasons for it as far exceed those of the other as Glasgow exceeds Renfrew". The Commission of Assembly agreed. MacLaurin went to Glasgow and, as the Moderate party had anticipated, he soon found himself on opposite sides to Neil Campbell (from 1728 Principal of Glasgow University) as, for example, in the heresy trial of Professor John Simson, the first notable heretic of the reformed Church of Scotland. However, in addition to leading the Popular party in matters such as the Simson trial,[8] MacLaurin

6   SRO, CH. 2/546/8, Minutes of the Presbytery of Dunbarton, 3 July 1722, p. 96.
7   SRO, CH. 1/2/46, Assembly papers, f. 253-277: Transportation of John MacLaurin from Luss to Glasgow, 10 July 1722. Reasons from commissioners from Glasgow.
8   H. F. Henderson, *The Religious Controversies of Scotland* (Edinburgh, 1905), p. 14.

took seriously the injunction of the Commission of Assembly who, on agreeing to his translation, urged him "to take special inspection of the Highland people in Glasgow" administering the sacraments, catechising and preaching to them. From 1721 until his death in 1754 MacLaurin preached every month in Gaelic and devoted a considerable proportion of his time and his means to the welfare of the Highlanders.[9, 10]

2.1.2. Ingram Street Gaelic Chapel 1770-1839

Following John MacLaurin's death the pastoral care of the Highlanders was undertaken by the Glasgow Highland Society working in conjunction with the S.S.P.C.K. In 1767 the Gaelic Chapel Society — an offshoot of the Glasgow Highland Society — undertook the erection of a Gaelic Chapel and a building, originally known as the Highland Church and later as Ingram Street Gaelic Chapel, was opened on Back Cow Loan on 18 February 1770. The original structure had a short life for in 1779 because of "the insufficiency of the walls and roof" it was largely demolished and rebuilt.[11] The rebuilt structure lasted almost sixty years. Then, to the great benefit of the congregation's finances, it was sold for redevelopment and a new church, which was to take the name St Columba's Gaelic Church, was built on Hope Street.

9　J. Gillies, 'Some Account of the Life and Character of McLaurin' in *The Works of the Rev. John MacLaurin* (2 vols., Edinburgh, 1860) ed. W. H. Goold, p. xv.

10　The recently published *Dictionary of Scottish Church History & Theology* (ed N. M. de S. Cameron, Edinburgh 1993) includes references to the notable Ramshorn Parish ministers John Anderson and John MacLaurin but few indeed of the ministers associated with Glasgow's Gaelic churches are listed in the Dictionary. As regards Highland ministers and Highland religion generally, there are useful articles reflecting to some extent the standpoint of the contributors.

11　*Extracts from the Records of the Burgh of Glasgow 1770-1780*, ed. R. Renwick (Glasgow, 1912), 521-4.

The first minister of Ingram Street Gaelic Chapel was the Rev Hugh McDiarmid, ordained to the charge in 1772. In 1780 he achieved what, to the popular mind, was seen as being the ultimate ambition of every chapel minister — a present-ation to a parish church, a situation which considerably enhanced a minister's emoluments and his status both in the church and in the community. The appointee saw it as being "called to a greater sphere of usefulness". Hugh McDiarmid went to the Parish of Arrocher. Six months later he resigned from Arrocher having been offered the even more 'useful' living of Comrie where he remained until his death in 1801[12]. He was succeeded in Ingram Street by the Rev John Fraser.[13] Inducted in 1783, Fraser, in turn, was elevated to the parish ministry at Kiltarlity in 1792. Now a change in mood became evident in the Ingram Street pulpit. Fraser was followed by Angus MacIntosh of Moy, a Highlander of commanding presence and equipped with a magnificent voice. He enjoyed a reputation for "piety and ministerial excellencies" unsurpassed by any of his contemporaries.[14] Although Angus MacIntosh's ministry in Glasgow was brief (he stayed less than five years) it was by all accounts conspicuously successful and uncompro-misingly evangelical with the result that many of his congrega-tion adopted evangelical views and would not agree to the election of a minister of Moderate tendencies to succeed him. As it happened the man the chapel managers had in mind to succeed MacIntosh was unquestionably of the Moderate persuasion. This was the Rev. John McLaurin (no relation to

12 For the Rev. Hugh M'Diarmid see *Fasti Ecclesiae Scoticanae* vol. 4 (Edinburgh, 1923), p. 263.
13 For the Rev. John Fraser see *Fasti Ecclesiae Scoticanae* vol. 6 (Edinburgh, 1926), p. 469.
14 For a description of the Rev. Angus MacIntosh see *Sketches of Religion and and Revivals of Religion in the North Highlands during the 18th century* by the Rev. Angus MacGillivray (Glasgow, 1904), pp. 34-39. See also *Memorials of the Life and Ministry of Charles Calder MacKintosh, D.D.* edited by the Rev. Wm Taylor (Edinburgh, 1870).

John MacLaurin of the Ramshorn Kirk) who was at that time assistant at Comrie to the former minister of Ingram Street, Hugh McDiarmid. McLaurin and McDiarmid were two of a kind, equally at home in the austere atmosphere of the Gaelic Chapel or in the convivial atmosphere of the Gaelic Club. This duality of outlook they shared with some of the Chapel's leading managers, notably Malcolm McGilvra, a woollen and linen merchant of considerable standing in Glasgow's commercial life, George MacIntosh, a formidable entrepreneur in footwear and dyestuffs whose son James devised the MacIntosh waterproof, James Campbell a saddler, and John Campbell a watchmaker.[15]

In October 1797 the Ingram Street Chapel managers led by Malcolm McGilvra petitioned the Presbytery for the induction of the Rev John McLaurin as successor to Angus MacIntosh. They produced documents attesting his election by the congregation but their plea was opposed by a counterpetition, the signatories to which included three men who had been made office-bearers by Angus MacIntosh. The counterpetition claimed that the election had been rigged and that "various improprieties took place and undue means were used" resulting in a narrow victory for McLaurin over the people's candidate, the Rev. John Mackenzie of Aberdeen Gaelic Chapel. Mackenzie, it was said, had been subjected to character assassination by the managers, it having been "industriously reported that he was a Democrat and this report was continued to be propagated in the face of unquestionable evidence to the contrary". The way in which the election had been rigged was said to be "the common topic of conversation in the city of Glasgow".[16] In a chapel election, voting rights

15 For a description of the Gaelic Club and its members see *Glasgow and Its Clubs* by John Strang, 2nd edition revised, corrected and enlarged (Glasgow, 1857), pp. 106-123.

16 SRO, CH. 2/171/15, Minutes of the Presbytery of Glasgow, 4 October 1797, p. 148ff. For MacLaurin see *Fasti Ecclesiae Scoticanae* vol. 3 (Edinburgh, 1920), p. 437.

were restricted to those who had been seat-holders for a least twelve months and it may well have been that a majority of the "hearers" wanted Mackenzie as minister but the Presbytery, in that time of political ferment and revolutionary tendency, viewed with alarm the prospect of a man of democratic outlook achieving a position of influence in the city. They voted for the induction of McLaurin. Moderate and Evangelical affiliations doubtless also influenced the Presbytery's decision. Robert Balfour, minister of the Outer High Kirk (the East Parish) and leader of the Evangelical party in the Presbytery dissented from the decision but did not pursue an appeal and McLaurin was inducted in January 1798. He remained in Ingram Street until his death in 1835 when he was succeeded by the most famous of the Gaelic ministers, Norman Macleod, *Caraid nan Gaidheal*, whose pastorate will be referred to in a later section.

Before Norman Macleod went from Campsie to Ingram Street the chapel managers were already negotiating with a view to realising the capital value of their Ingram Street site and moving the church Westward to cheaper ground. A defective title-deed requiring amendment by Act of Parliament delayed the sale but in 1837 the chapel was sold to the British Linen Bank for £12,000. The following year the foundation stone of a new church was laid on Hope Street.

2.1.3. Duke Street Gaelic Chapel 1798-1843

Even before McLaurin's induction took place, the Evangelical party in the Ingram Street Chapel began proceedings to establish a second Gaelic Chapel, formidable though the obstacles to such an undertaking were. Because of the rapid increase in Glasgow's Gaelic population and the general enthusiasm for the recruitment of an evangelical preacher, raising the necessary funds was relatively straightforward and there was no shortage of building sites in the expanding city. A more troublesome matter was the need to obtain the agreement of the Presbytery and the Assembly without which no minister of the Established Church could officiate in a new chapel. A petition for the approval of Presbytery came before that court in March 1798 when the need for a second chapel was urged on the grounds of insufficient accommodation in the Ingram Street Chapel for the expanding Gaelic population. The petition affirmed that 600 subscribers had come forward and pledged half the cost of the new building which was estimated to be £1400. The Presbytery deferred a decision to allow for consultation with interested parties such as the heritors and magistrates and when the matter came before the next meeting, only the casting vote of the Moderator allowed the petition to proceed to the General Assembly.[17] The Assembly gave its approval and in October 1798 the Rev. John Mackenzie, minister of Aberdeen Gaelic Chapel, was duly inducted as first minister of Duke Street Gaelic Chapel. Of the two Gaelic churches Duke Street was the larger having 1263 sittings.

It is to be noted that none of the managers of Ingram Street Gaelic Chapel appeared in support of the petition for a second chapel.[18] Although Duke Street congregation was able to claim one manufacturer (John Macintosh) and one merchant (Daniel McKellar) in its first Kirk Session, the remaining office-bearers were all from the artisan class and in that, they

---

17   SRO, CH. 2/171/15, Minutes of the Presbytery of Glasgow, 9 May 1798, p. 168.
18   The contrary is affirmed by C. W. J. Withers, *Highland Clubs and Chapels: Glasgow's Gaelic Community in the Eighteenth Century*, SCOTTISH GEOGRAPHICAL MAGAZINE vol. 101, p. 23 where it is stated that (Malcolm) McGilvra and (George) MacIntosh supported the petition. But McGilvra is not referred to in the minutes as supporting the petition and the MacIntosh referred to is a John MacIntosh and not the dye manufacturer George MacIntosh.

reflected the complexion of the congregation. One of the most notable of the managers of Ingram Street Chapel was the Ross-shire-born George MacIntosh who made his fortune by exploiting the manufacture of "cudbear", a dye used for colouring silk and wool. The industry was associated with a highly objectionable smell and it was pursued by MacIntosh in premises which he built across the Molendinar burn, in a 17 acre estate at Easter Craigs. Here, in his Dunchattan works, surrounded by a ten foot high wall, he "established a colony of Highland workmen some of whom are said to have lived and died there without learning the English language"[19] MacIntosh was disposed to recruit Highlanders as his employees and possibly many of them thought it politic, in the interests of their employment, to put in an appearance at Ingram Street Chapel. However, although MacIntosh did not identify himself with the Duke Street petition there is no evidence to suggest that he was actively opposed to it and, interestingly, the chapel was erected not far from his Dunchatten works. The site was on the South side of Duke Street near its junction with the High Street.

John Mackenzie remained in Duke Street Chapel for ten years before he took the unusual step of returning to his former congregation in Aberdeen. In 1810 he was followed by the entertaining and hugely popular David Carment. If reasons, however flimsy, could be adduced for considering John Mackenzie to be a dangerous democrat, and therefore a threat to the ordered structure of society, no such allegations could be made against Carment. On the contrary he was stigmatised as being in the opposite camp. In those days, when the whiff of revolution wafting from across the English Channel was very much in the air, there were some who identified radicalism with

19   George Eyre-Todd, *History of Glasgow* (Glasgow, 1934), vol. 3, p. 304.

infidelity and impiety. To be a radical was to be an infidel and some churchmen saw it as their duty to oppose the radical movement. Carment, a man with a highly developed instinct for battle, was one of those. His pamphleteering so incensed the supporters of the new movement that his life was threatened and for his own safety he had to leave Glasgow until tempers cooled.[20] This episode did nothing to lessen his popularity with the Duke Street chapelgoers who, on his return, so thronged the building that boards were placed across the aisles between the pews to increase the seating capacity. Nor did his conservative views prevent him from showing compassion to the individual in need. He was instrumental in forming an association in Glasgow called "The Highland Strangers Society". In such ways David Carment demonstrated his commitment both to the truth, as he saw it, and to society. It was during his ministry that Duke Street chapel attained its greatest prosperity but in 1822 Carment received a presentation to the parish of Rosskeen which offer he readily accepted, carrying as it did the right to a place in the Church's judicatories This considerably extended his sphere of influence, notably in the General Assembly, and he made good use of his opportunities.[21]

Robert Clark, Carment's successor, was cast in quite the opposite mould. Like John Mackenzie he was called to Duke Street from Aberdeen Gaelic Chapel. Solemn, morose and a chronic invalid, his pastorate was sustained with the help of assistants, one of whom was the eccentric genius 'Rabbi' Duncan whose gifts were not uniformly appreciated in Duke

20 Samuel Carment, *Memoir of the Rev. James Carment* with an introduction by the Rev. Alex Beith (Dalkeith, 1886), p.3.
21 For a description of the Rev. David Carment see *Disruption Worthies: a memorial of 1843* edited by the Rev. J. A. Wylie (Edinburgh, 1881) pp. 147-151; and Donald Sage, *Memorabilia Domestica* (Wick, 1899), 2nd edition p. 283 and p. 294.

Street.[22] Clark gave eleven years of service in Glasgow. By 1831, if not sooner, his congregation were longing for a change. According to a contemporary account Robert Clark was "in feeble health" and his pulpit ministrations were not "suited to the strong appetite of his thoughtful Highlanders".[23] However, this assessment may do less than justice to his intellectual ability. In 1834 he returned to his native Sutherlandshire as minister of the *quoad sacra* parish of Kinlochbervie. The presentation to this parish was given by the Crown but it did not have the support of the people who instead had set their hearts on the Rev. Archibald Cook of Berridale and Bruan. Cook had indicated his willingness to accept the presentation if awarded it. Only ten persons signed the call to Clark although more would have done so had they not been intimidated.[24] Surprisingly perhaps, the Presbytery of Tongue, the ministers of which were to come out at the Disruption, intruded the Crown's presentee on the parish whereupon the body of the people withdrew from the congregation. Having had that experience it is not to be wondered at that Robert Clark, despite his commitment to the Evangelical Party, remained in the Established Church in 1843.[25] Clearly there was nowhere for him to go.

When Clark left Duke Street Chapel all three of Glasgow's Gaelic churches were vacant. Lewis Rose of Nigg was strongly supported by a section of both Duke Street and Hope Street but he withdrew his name from consideration by Hope Street and accepted a call to Duke Street.

22   Wm. Knight, *Colloquia peripatetica* (Edinburgh, 1879), 5th edition p. lvii.
23   David Brown, *Life of John Duncan* (Edinburgh, 1872), p. 251.
24   Alex Macrae, *Kinlochbervie* (Tongue, Sutherland, ND), p. 46.
25   For further information on Robert Clark see Alex Macrae, *Kinlochbervie*.

2.1.4. Kirkfield (Gorbals) Gaelic Chapel 1813 - 1834

One of the first chapels-of-ease to be erected in Glasgow was built in Buchan Street, Gorbals, in 1730. On being disjoined from the Barony of Govan in 1771 this chapel became Gorbals Parish Church. In 1811 a new church was built in Carlton Place and the vacated building in Buchan Street became the subject of a petition from certain residents in Gorbals led by one James Macfarlane, a shoemaker. The petition affirmed that "a considerable proportion of the people in Gorbals are Highlanders who best understand and are most attached to the Gaelic language". It averred that many of them had been disappointed in making application for seats in the existing Gaelic Chapels (Ingram Street and Duke Street) and it requested that the Buchan Street building be reopened as a Gaelic Chapel.[26] The Presbytery concurred with the petition and the Assembly of 1813 approved a constitution (or licence) for the Kirkfield (Gorbals) Gaelic Chapel, erected for the benefit of Gaelic-speaking people on the South side of the city. However the terms in which the constitution was drawn, recognised the new congregation simply as a chapel-of-ease and not as a specifically Gaelic chapel. When a petition for another Gaelic Chapel (Hope Street) was framed in 1823, one of the arguments employed was that since the constitution of the Gorbals Chapel made no reference to Gaelic, there was no guarantee that Gaelic would remain a permanent feature of the worship of that congregation. Subsequent events showed that this concern was fully justified.

The Kirkfield chapel called as its first (and, as it turned out, only) Gaelic-speaking minister, the Rev. John Mackenzie who in 1809 had returned to Aberdeen Gaelic Chapel after serving as first minister of Duke Street chapel. In Kirkfield he

26   SRO, CH. 2/171/16, Minutes of the Presbytery of Glasgow, 5 May 1813, p. 313.

enjoyed a stipend of £150 and preached in both Gaelic and English. In 1823, pleading ill-health, he applied for an assistant and successor and his son, Kenneth, was elected. Although the father died before the son was ordained, Kenneth was eventually inducted to the charge and he remained there until 1834 when he was translated to the parish of Borrowstouness (Bo'ness). It seems that Kenneth was of a cautious temperament. Tradition has it that the patron of Bo'ness invited the parishioners to state a preference for one of three men, any one of whom he was willing to have as minister. The men, in turn, were invited to specify what benefits they would bring to the parishioners. The first offered to give plots of the manse glebe land to the cottars. The second vowed "to do something" but declined to say what. Kenneth Mackenzie said he would "make no promises"; but he was elected by a large majority. [27]

It would appear that the Kirkfield Chapel ceased to be a Gaelic charge on the induction of Kenneth Mackenzie in 1824. Brought up in Glasgow and Aberdeen, he would have had no incentive to acquire Gaelic and, at a time when divinity students such as Alex Stewart (latterly of Cromarty), the son of the Gaelic Bible translator Dr Alex Stewart of Moulin and Dingwall, had to withdraw to a remote Highland glen in order to gain proficiency in Gaelic,[28] it is improbable that Kenneth Mackenzie would have developed a facility in that language in the Gorbals manse. Certainly Norman Macleod of the Barony, son of Caraid nan Gaidheal, learned no Gaelic in the Ingram Street manse, or for that matter, anywhere else. Generally speaking, Gaelic

27 Thomas J Salmon, *Borrowstounness and District*. (Edinburgh, 1913).
28 Alex Beith, Biographical notice prefacing *The Tree of Promise* by the Rev. Alex. Stewart. Cromarty (Edinburgh, 1864), p. xxviii. See also Alex Beith, *A Highland Tour* (Edinburgh, 1874) 2nd edition, pp. 247-264.

ministers made no attempt to ensure that their own offspring learned Gaelic and it is unlikely that Kenneth Mackenzie fared differently in the Gorbals. At his induction to Kirkfield, the Presbytery did not make the usual provision for a Gaelic preacher to conduct the service in Gaelic. Indeed it is at this time (1824) that the Presbytery minutes cease to refer to the charge as the Gaelic Chapel, Gorbals, calling it instead simply Kirkfield. Significantly the Presbytery minutes carry no reference to a resolution to discontinue Gaelic ministry in Gorbals. Since there was no enactment regarding Gaelic in the Kirkfield constitution it was within the power of the congregation to take any such decision and the Presbytery tacitly concurred.

In 1834, Kenneth Mackenzie was succeeded by the Rev. Jonathan Rankin Anderson under whose vigorous, but quarrelsome, leadership[29] the congregation, in 1842, moved to a new church known as John Knox's located at the junction of Surrey Street and Bedford Street. In the course of construction of this building, J R Anderson anticipated the events of 1843 and when the Disruption took place Anderson and his congregation joined the Free Church taking their building with them — one of a handful of instances where a Disruption congregation actually possessed a title to the building in which they worshipped. In 1853, Anderson, on account of his attacks on the integrity of his fellow ministers, was deposed from the ministry of the Free Church and he, along with some influential members of his congregation, formed an independent chapel (Knox Tabernacle) which, in 1896, was received into the Free Presbyterian Church. In John Knox's Anderson was succeeded by Archibald Bannatyne who left Oban Gaelic Church because

---

29 For some account of his ministry see *Rev. Jonathan Rankin Anderson: Defender of the Faith or Accuser of the Brethren* by I. R. MacDonald, Monthly Record of The Free Church of Scotland, November 1988.

his Gaelic was so poor.[30] John Knox's, although not a Gaelic congregation, retained a strong Highland element and, up until the appointment of the Rev John Buchan in 1888 (father of the first Lord Tweedsmuir and of O Douglas), the congregation was pastored by ministers of a very conservative outlook. In 1911 when John Buchan died, John Knox congregation was merged with Tradeston, itself an amalgam formed from another Gaelic congregation (Argyle) which in 1842 occupied the vacated Kirkfield Chapel.

2.1.5 Hope Street Gaelic Chapel 1824 - 1843

Glasgow's fourth Gaelic Chapel was constituted in 1824 but it had its origin in a disputed settlement in Duke Street Gaelic church in 1823. When the translation of the Rev David Carment to Rosskeen left Duke Street vacant, the congregation drew up a list of four candidates, the first being the Rev. Robert Clark minister of Aberdeen Gaelic Chapel, and the second Duncan McCaig, missionary at Fort William. In the election Clark was successful. That same month a meeting took place in Provands Hall at which it was agreed to petition the Presbytery of Glasgow for permission to form another Gaelic congregation. The ostensible reason given was that this proposed congregation would be for the benefit of Argyllshire Highlanders whose Gaelic dialect was not catered for in the existing churches where the preachers were all from the Northern Highlands. The petitioners went so far as to claim that "the difference between the dialects of the West and North Highlands is so great that the natives of the one frequently do not understand at all the language spoken in the other".[31]

---

30 Norman C. Macfarlane, *Rev. Donald John Martin* (Edinburgh, 1914) pp. 179-180.
31 SRO, CH. 16/3/1/1, Hope Street Gaelic Chapel Managers' Minutes: Petition of March 1823 to Presbytery of Glasgow.

The Presbytery consulted the other Gaelic congregations about this proposal and found them to be uniformly opposed to it. All of them had unlet sittings, two of them were burdened with debt and any new congregation, it was argued, would only injure the existing ones. The managers of Gorbals Gaelic Chapel which had a debt of £1252 and no fewer than 530 of its 1086 sittings unlet, offered the most cogent criticism. They pointed out that the most homogenous Argyllshire Gaelic congregations in the country — Greenock and Rothesay — both had North country ministers and no preachers were more popular among the Gaelic people of Argyllshire than Kenneth Bayne in Greenock and David Fraser in Rothesay. They went on to say that the dialect argument was an excuse rather than a reason, for "if the recent election of a minister for the Gaelic Chapel Duke Street had been unanimous the Presbytery would not have been troubled with this application".[32] The correctness of this view would seem to be borne out by the circumstance that when permission was eventually granted, the 'Argyllshire' congregation gave a call to Duncan McCaig, the defeated candidate in the Duke Street election. Moreover, the list of preachers submitted by the new congregation for Presbytery approval included more North country men than Argyllshire men.[33] In the event, Duncan McCaig declined the call. Alex Beith, Hope Street's first minister, did have Argyllshire connections but he left Hope Street after only two years and his successor, Adam Gun, was a Caithness man. It would seem, therefore, that the managers of Gorbals Gaelic Chapel were as perceptive in diagnosing the circumstances surrounding the plea for another congregation as they were in anticipating the consequences.

32   SRO, CH. 1/2/145, Assembly Papers for 1823. Petition from Managers of Gorbals Gaelic Chapel 1 April 1823.
33   SRO, CH. 2/171/17, Minutes of the Presbytery of Glasgow, June 1824, p. 363

They had warned that "a new chapel would only tend to ruin those already built, and especially this one", the greatest proportion of the Gorbals congregation being from the West Highlands. Only a few months were to elapse before the Gorbals Chapel gave up the attempt to compete on the Gaelic scene.

In 1824 the Hope Street congregation erected their chapel at the Northern corner of Hope Street and Melville Street (now Gordon Street). It was not without its problems; the roof leaked, the walls were porous and the chimneys did not draw. Duncan McCaig having declined a call, the congregation called the Rev. Alex Beith of Oban Gaelic Church, a man highly gifted both as a speaker and as a writer, incidentally a trait that was to reappear in his grandson, Major-General Ian Hay the best-selling author of the First World War. The Presbytery approved the call to Beith who was to have a stipend of £300 and, as was usual in a Gaelic charge, they authorised the Gaelic-speaking Dr Daniel Dewar of the Tron Church to preach and preside on the occasion. The appointment of Dr Dewar to this office was objected to by the irascible minister of Campsie, the Rev. James Lapslie who dissented for reasons which he undertook to submit to the next meeting of Presbytery. Sadly Lapslie died on his way to that meeting of Presbytery and the reasons remain undiscoverable. Beith's ministry although brief was fruitful. His successor, Adam Gun superintendent of schools with Inverness Education Authority, was elected by 202 votes to one. He officiated from 1827 until 1835 when he left under a cloud and, in 1836, he was succeeded by the Rev Hector McNeil. Mr McNeil's ministry failed to draw the crowds and taking into consideration the thin attendance the managers "unanimously agreed to leave it to Mr McNeil's discretion how to act in the matter but recommended that he should preach himself once a month". [34] However the congregation had to make do with him until 1841 when, following a decision to reduce his stipend from £300 to £250, he left for Campbeltown. Perhaps as an expression of their gratitude for this gesture, he had no sooner left than he was invited to return as visiting preacher at the next Communion.

The election of a successor to McNeil was a contentious affair but eventually Walter MacGilvray, an Islay man officiating in another Glasgow church, was elected. MacGilvray was a scholarly man who, by virtue of his marriage to a daughter of Sir William Hooker, director of Kew Gardens, was within Charles Darwin's circle of friends. He was admitted to Hope Street in June 1842 with the ubiquitous Dr Daniel Dewar, by now Principal of Marishal College Aberdeen, presiding. The noise of battle over the Intrusion issue was now becoming ever more clamorous and it is inconceivable that an induction service could have passed without reference to it but on the day of decision, and contrary to all expectations, it was MacGilvray and not Dewar who sided with the Free Church. His congregation backed him to a man and Hope Street Gaelic Chapel became Hope Street Free Gaelic Church. [35]

2.1.6 Argyle Gaelic Church 1842-1843

When Hope Street became vacant following the departure of Hector McNeil in 1841, the congregation drew up a list of eight candidates to fill the vacancy. Of the eight, only two commanded serious support, Walter MacGilvray who was eventually elected, and Archibald MacDougall a native of Tarbert Lochfyne who two years earlier had become a licentiate of the

34   SRO, CH. 16/3/1/2, Hope Street Gaelic Chapel Managers' Minutes, 24 May 1837.
35   For a brief history of Hope Street Church 1824-1971 see *The Hope Street Story* by Evan G. Macdonald. 22pp. Published by the congregation 1971.

church at the age of 38. MacGilvray was obviously favoured by the chapel management and voting members supported him by 115 to 28. But MacDougall had additional support among a section who were not entitled to vote and a protest movement developed. The leaders of this movement complained to the Presbytery of irregularities in the election procedure but they did not press their opposition beyond the point of lodging a complaint. However, in June 1842 a petition was submitted to the Presbytery on behalf of "a great number of individual members of Hope Street" requesting that they be allowed to form another congregation in connection with the Established Church. In September the Presbytery, by a narrow vote of 19 to 15, agreed to allow this dissentient group to engage a separate preacher.[36] This was the origin of Glasgow's fifth Gaelic congregation connected with the Established Church. They first met for public worship in a hall on George Street but when J R Anderson moved his congregation to the new John Knox Church in the autumn of 1842, the Hope Street dissidents moved into the vacated Kirkfield church on Buchan Street.[37] In February 1843 the new Gaelic congregation petitioned the Presbytery to settle the Rev. Archibald MacDougall as their pastor. The Presbytery agreed but the Disruption intervened and Argyle was never officially a settled charge of the Established Church. MacDougall's ordination and induction was eventually carried through by the Free Presbytery of Glasgow.

36 SRO, CH. 2/171/20, Minutes of the Presbytery of Glasgow, Sept 1842, p. 465..
37 SRO, CH. 3/1298/3, Argyle Free Gaelic Kirk Session Minutes, 6 June 1883.

2.2   Scots Independent and United Secession Church. Rev John Campbell 1810-1828

Among the reasons advanced in the 1823 petition for the erection of Hope Street Gaelic Church, it was said that there was "only one chapel in Glasgow in which a clergyman from the West Highlands officiates and it is always full". The chapel in question was an Old Scots Independent church on Nicolson Street, Gorbals. It was a substantial building having 910 sittings. The preacher was John Campbell, a native of Lochgilphead.[38] As a divinity student he left the Established Church to join the Haldane Mission. His first charge was in the West Port, Dundee where he was associated with Niel Douglas, a minister of the Relief Church, himself a very appealing Gaelic preacher.[39]

The Secession Gaelic church had a complicated ancestry. About the year 1800 the Haldanes acquired a circus building in Jamaica Street and transformed it into their Glasgow Tabernacle with the Rev. Greville Ewing as minister. When the Haldanes adopted Baptist views, Ewing, in 1810, moved his congregation to West Nile Street but a number of them, possibly the Highland element, remained behind and called John Campbell from Dundee. In 1814 Campbell and his congregation took a site in Nicholson Street, Gorbals, and built an independent church where he exercised a very Presbyterian ministry; so much so, in fact, that in 1821 the congregation was admitted into the newly formed United Secession Church

---

38   For information on the Rev. John Campbell, see R. Small, *History of the Congregations of the United Presbyterian Church from 1733 to 1900* (2 vols Edinburgh, 1904), 2, pp. 61-62.

39   J MacInnes, *The Evangelical Movement in the Highlands of Scotland. 1688-1800* (Aberdeen, 1951), p. 142. See also in relation to Niel Douglas' turbulent history, G. Struthers, *The History of the Rise, Progress and Principles of the Relief Church* (Glasgow, 1843) Appendix X.

to become the sixth congregation of that church in Glasgow. John Campbell's Gaelic ministry in that church was highly popular but Gaelic preaching there terminated with his death in 1828 at the age of 59. Subsequently the church was used by various congregations each in turn expanding and moving Westwards. In this century the site was occupied by the Reformed Presbyterian Church.[40]

2.3   Congregational Union. Fraser Hall 1825-30 and Brown Street 1830-36.

The Congregational Church also had a Gaelic preacher in the person of the Rev Edward Campbell who was called to a church constituted in 1825 and which met in Fraser's Hall, King Street near the Tron Gate. In 1830 the congregation moved to Brown Street on the Broomielaw and in 1841 it crossed the river to the Nicholson Street church mentioned above. In 1866 it resumed its migratory existence moving first to Kingston Free Church, then to Eglinton Street and in 1936 to Fenwick Road in Giffnock. However its Gaelic phase was restricted to the ministry of Edward Campbell in Fraser's Hall and Brown Street. When he died in 1836 the Gaelic services were discontinued as being no longer necessary.[41]

---

40 John Ord, *The Story of the Barony of Gorbals* (Paisley, 1919), p. 109.
41 Harry Escott, *A History of Scottish Congregationalism* (Glasgow, 1960), p. 300.

2.4   The Roman Catholic Church.   Glasgow Catholic Highland Mission

Dr Webster estimated, in the census which he conducted in 1755, that there were 265 Roman Catholics in Edinburgh but only five in all of Lanarkshire and Renfrewshire. However, that was soon to change and, interestingly, in the resurgent Catholic Church formed in Glasgow at the end of the 18th century, Gaelic speakers were probably in the majority. As it happened, Edinburgh anticipated Glasgow in the provision of Gaelic services in the Catholic Church as in the Protestant Church. (The Edinburgh Catholic Highland Chapel in Blackfriars Wynd off the High Street was roughly contemporary with the Edinburgh Gaelic Chapel on Castle Wynd. The Blackfriars Chapel was rebuilt in 1780 by the then resident priest, the Rev. Robert Menzies, a Gaelic speaker from Perthshire.[42] Following his death in 1791 difficulty was experienced in finding a Gaelic-speaking successor and prior to the appointment of the Rev. Alex Macdonald of Crieff, the vacancy was partly supplied by the Gaelic-speaking Father Alex Macdonald, later Bishop of Kingston, Canada, and partly by the Rev. James Robertson.[43])

In Glasgow in the 1770's a score or so of Catholics met in a room on the High Street and, later, at the East end of the Gallowgate Street. Both places were wrecked in anti-popery riots in 1778 and the group then met in a small upstairs room in a close off the Saltmarket opposite the Bridgegate.[44] Here they continued until 1791 when premises in Mitchell St. were fitted up as a temporary church. It was at this time that

---

42   W. J Anderson, *The Edinburgh Highland Chapel and the Rev. Robert Menzies,* THE INNES REVIEW vol. 17 (1966) pp. 195-198.

43   The Scottish Catholic Directory for 1838 p. 49.

44   James Walsh, *History of the Catholic Church in Scotland* (Glasgow, 1874), p. 526..

Glasgow obtained, in the person of Father Alex Macdonald, its first resident priest since the Reformation. This Alex Macdonald was a Glen Urquhart man who played an active role in obtaining employment in Glasgow for Gaelic-speaking Catholic Highlanders. In 1792 when there was a scarcity of labour in the city, Father Macdonald is said to have brought 600 Highlanders to Glasgow, he himself acting as their interpreter and spiritual adviser.[45] He persuaded the manufacturers who employed these men to act as cautioners for the £40 rent of the Mitchell Street premises and the Catholic Chapel was opened in October 1792 with a congregation of 200 persons. The employers also agreed to pay £30 per annum for the priest's support.[46] Macdonald, however, was a man of shifting enthusiasms and in 1794 when war with France forced a cutback in Glasgow's exports to the Continent and the Highlanders were laid-off, Father Macdonald raised a regiment known as the Glengarry Fencibles and recruited his unemployed parishioners as soldiers.[47] When the regiment was disbanded in 1802, the Fencibles emigrated to Canada under the command of their erstwhile chaplain who was later to become Bishop of Kingston.

Although Macdonald had laid the foundation for the Glasgow Catholic Highland Mission it clearly needed a less restless priest to nurture it. In 1795 Bishop Chisholm, vicar apostolic in the Highland District, writing to his counterpart in the Lowland District stressed the need for a Gaelic man. There were, he said, no fewer than 500 persons in the Mission, "Irish included, among whom scarce a score could be had that did

---

45 *Ibid.*, p.541.
46 Alex MacWilliam, *The Glasgow Mission 1792-1799*, THE INNES REVIEW vol. 4, pp. 84-91.
47 George Eyre-Todd, *History of Glasgow* (Glasgow, 1934), vol. 3, p. 369.

not speak Gaelic".[48] However, the priest appointed was John
Farquharson, a Banffshire man but not a Gaelic speaker. He
instituted a building programme and opened a new chapel in
Boar Head Lane in October 1797. In a letter to a brother
minister in 1799, Farquharson made reference to the founding
father, the Rev. Alex Macdonald, "My predecessor is with me
just now thundering Gaelic sermons to his quondam flock".[49]
Clearly Gaelic preaching still had an appeal for Glasgow
Catholics but its supply would seem to have been restricted to
'guest appearances'. In 1805, the Rev. Andrew Scott, another
non-Gaelic man, succeeded John Farquharson and although
the Catholic population of Glasgow was increasing by leaps
and bounds, the Catholic authorities appear thereafter not to
have employed a priest with a specific remit to minister to Gaelic
speakers. The problem of coping with the enormous influx of
Irish Catholics distracted attention from the needs of the
native Highlanders although as late as 1826 a Highland priest
still made occasional visits to Glasgow to give Confession to
the few Catholic Gaelic-speaking Highlanders in the city.[50]

48   Alex MacWilliam, *The Glasgow Mission1792-1799*, THE INNES REVIEW vol. 4,
     pp. 84-91
49   *Ibid.*
50   Christine Johnson, *Developments in the Roman Catholic Church in Scotland 1789-1829*
     (Edinburgh, 1983) p.24.

3   THE POST-DISRUPTION HISTORY OF PRE-DISRUPTION GAELIC CONGREGATIONS

3.1   1843 and the parting of the ways

In 1843 four Gaelic congregations survived in Glasgow viz., the original Gaelic Chapel founded on Ingram Street in 1770 but relocated in new premises on Hope Street in 1839 and thereafter known as St Columba Gaelic Church; Duke Street Gaelic Chapel (1798), Hope Street Gaelic Chapel (1824) and the recently constituted Argyle Gaelic Church (1842). In 1843 each of these congregations had to consider its position in relation to the Disruption.

The Disruption was the culmination of a long-standing conflict between the Evangelical Party in the Church of Scotland and the heritors or patrons who, being legally responsible for the maintenance of the parish churches, enjoyed as a *quid pro quo* the right to chose the parish minister. At one time the right to nominate the minister was tempered by a process of congregational consultation but latterly some patrons sought to impose their nominees without regard to their acceptability to the people. Contemporaneously with this development the Evangelical Party was gaining strength in the Assembly and, with a confidence founded on the strength born of numbers together with a categorical conviction in the rightness of their cause, the Evangelicals embarked on a policy of confrontation. They affirmed that the Church was not obliged to confer the spiritual office of ordination or induction on prospective ministers whom the Church judged to be unsuitable because they lacked the support of the people and so they refused to administer the required consecration. Then when the Civil Courts, acting at the behest of the patrons, insisted that the Church must ordain appointees irrespective of their acceptability to the people, the Evangelicals protested that the spiritual liberties of the Church were being made subject to intolerable interference and that they had no alternative but to withdraw from the Establishment. And so, in May 1843, the Church of Scotland, Free, came into being. It claimed to be the same church as that which it had left, a church adhering to the same Confession of Faith, loyal to the same principles, differing only inasmuch as in the discharge of its spiritual functions, it was to be subservient to no other authority than the will of God as understood by the collective mind of the Church. The movement gained the support of 474 ministers of the Church of Scotland, less than its promoters had hoped for but still a remarkable demonstration of loyalty to a spiritual principle regardless of the material consequences. The ministers who signed away their rights to the substantial emoluments of the parish ministry maintained that their protest was against State interference in matters that belonged to the spiritual jurisdiction of the church. The Disruption was intended to be, not a disruption or division of the church, but a disruption of the link that bound the church to the State. The leaders had hoped that the church as a body would quit the Establishment. In the event of course, the Church of Scotland was not itself of one mind in the matter and because it did not act as one body in its reaction to State interference, it was inevitably rent in two. The Church of Scotland as by law established remained, and the Church of Scotland, Free, came into existence. In this situation the Gaelic congregations, like all the others, had to decide whether or not to quit the Establishment. Because of their nonparochial status none of them had been subject to ministerial intrusion from autocratic patrons and their attitude to the Disruption was largely determined by their ecclesiastical loyalties. Basically all of them were evangelical as were their ministers; but not all the Gaelic ministers were minded to leave the Establishment. Consequently some congregations had to consider their loyalty to their minister where that conflicted with their Evangelical Party sympathies. In the event, although the Gaelic congregations did not act in unison, there was a large measure of unanimity within each congregation with the result that none of them experienced any serious internal disruption. St Columba adhered to the Church of Scotland; the others joined the Free Church.

3.2   St Columba Gaelic Church of Scotland 1843-1900

Although the election of the Rev. Norman Macleod, minister of St Columba Gaelic Church, to the Moderatorship of the 1836 General Assembly — the first ever appointment of a Chapel-of-Ease minister to that office — was hailed by the Evangelicals as a triumph for their cause and party, St Columba had nevertheless the reputation of being "a stronghold of Moderatism",[1] and Norman Macleod was himself cast in the Moderate tradition — so much so that his son, Norman of the Barony, in his day an equally distinguished divine, has been described as "an hereditary Erastian".[2] When the crunch came in 1843, Norman Macleod stuck by the Established Church and such was his popularity with his own congregation that they, almost to a man, stayed with him. This was the only significant body of Glasgow Highlanders to remain in the Establishment and St Columba continued into the twentieth century to be Glasgow's focal point for Gaelic-speaking worshippers in the Church of Scotland. Its post Disruption history has been given book-length treatment from within its own ranks — the only one of Glasgow's Gaelic churches to be so favoured — and a further account is therefore unnecessary. Norman Macleod retired from his pulpit in St Columba's in

---

1   John C MacGregor, *The History of St Columba Parish Church* (Glasgow, 1935), p. 19.
2   John Macleod, *Scottish Theology* (Edinburgh, 1943), p. 301.

1855 and died in 1862.[3] His successors in the charge included his kinsman Dr Norman Macleod, latterly of Inverness High Church, Dr Robert Blair latterly of St John's Edinburgh, and Dr John Maclean, all of them noted Gaelic scholars [4] who contributed to the 1902 Revision of the Gaelic Bible.

At the end of the century the site occupied by St Columba's on Hope St., was required for the extension of Glasgow's railway system and, following the sale of the site, the final services to be held in 'the second temple' took place in May 1900. The foundation stone of the third church was laid in St Vincent Street in July 1902 and the new St Columba's was dedicated in September 1904. At the social function which accompanied the opening, the hoped-for prosperity of St Columba's was defined in terms that "it should be the centre of Celtic sentiment and Celtic aspirations in Glasgow".[5]

3.3   Duke Street Gaelic Church of Scotland 1843-1849

The minister of Duke Street Gaelic Chapel at the time of the Disruption was the Rev. Lewis Rose, a native of Nairnshire who, having been minister of Nigg in Easter Ross for upwards of seventeen years, was translated to Duke Street in 1836. Like his contemporary in St Columba's, Lewis Rose adhered to the Establishment in 1843 but unlike Norman Macleod, he failed to carry his congregation with him; the great majority joined the Free Church leaving a remnant in the Established Church. Within a matter of months Rose, sensing that the old Duke Street charge was no longer viable, accepted a presentation to the parish of Kincardine and Creich in the Presbytery of Tain. There, the Presbytery, supported by the arm of the law, inducted him much against the will of the people. Not until

---

3   For an account of the life of Dr Norman Macleod see J. N. Macleod, *Memorials of the Rev. Norman Macleod* (Edinburgh, 1898).

4   For a brief account of these men see Donald Mackinnon, *The Gaelic Bible and Psalter* (Dingwall, 1930), pp. 116-119.

5   John C MacGregor, ibid., p. 57.

1847 did the remnant in Duke Street succeed in their quest for another minister but his ministry was brief for John Mackay, who moved from Lochgilphead to Duke Street in 1847, resigned in 1849.

The Free Church section of the congregation made several unsuccessful attempts to claim the chapel on Duke Street but the House of Lords ruling on the legal ownership of *quoad sacra* churches which was delivered in February 1849 finally deprived the Free Church of any remaining hopes of obtaining these buildings and they abandoned their claim to Duke Street even although the Established Church had no further use for it. Following the resignation of John Mackay in 1849 the charge was suppressed and in 1851 the old Gaelic Church was bought by Father Peter Forbes who established St Vincent's Roman Catholic Mission in the building.[6] It was later demolished to allow for the extension of College Street Station goodsyard.

3. 4 Duke Street Free Gaelic Church 1843-1900

It seems likely that the Black Bull Inn was the first place of worship of the congregation which regrouped as the Free Protesting people of Duke Street. The Protestors had cherished hopes of repossessing their original chapel but with nothing happening to encourage them in that direction they decided on a different course. In March 1845 they petitioned the Presbytery "to be allowed to meet with said (i.e., Bridgegate) congregation in Bridgegate for public worship" and in May the Presbytery agreed to a petition (signed by upwards of 500 persons) from "the Highland congregation at present assembling for public worship in Bridgegate Church asking to be recognised as a fixed charge".[7] In September the Presbytery authorised the settlement of a minister and in January 1846 the congregation (still meeting in Bridgegate Church) elected John

6   Bernard Aspinwall, *A Glasgow Pastoral Plan 1855-1860* THE INNES REVIEW, 35, p. 33
7   SRO, CH. 3/146/34, Minutes of the Free Presbytery of Glasgow, 7 May 1845, p. 257.

Noble of Fodderty, the call being signed by 918 persons. In 1848 the Presbytery sanctioned a new site for the Duke Street Free Gaelic Church but John Noble died in 1849 and in 1850 the Presbytery learned that the congregation had parted with the site sanctioned by Presbytery and had acquired another near it without obtaining the consent of the Presbytery.[8] At the time the Presbytery refused to sanction any construction work but eventually after many delays, Duke Street Free Gaelic Church was erected in the 1850's between Waterloo Street and Bothwell Lane.

Following the untimely death of John Noble the congregation had many discouragements before they succeeded in getting another minister. A call had been sent to a highly-regarded Highland minister, the Rev George Mackay of the Free North Church, Inverness.[9] Mackay was reluctant to leave Inverness and although the Duke Street congregation appealed to the Assembly against the refusal of the Presbytery of Inverness to translate Mackay, the Assembly, taking note of Mackay's expressed preference, rejected the appeal.[10] Eventually, in 1854, the Rev. George G. Macleod was inducted to the Duke St congregation now meeting in Mains Street. Macleod was very active in outreach work among the destitute Highlanders but domestic difficulties — the death of his wife, his own shattered state of health and the care of a young and helpless family — led to an injudicious use of stimulants and his resignation from the charge in 1867.[11] However the Highland Committee continued to employ him in outreach work until his death in 1888.

In 1869 the Rev. Evan Gordon, a native of Kingussie, was translated from Grantown to Duke Street. The congregation

8   Ibid., SRO, CH. 3/146/35, 12 June 1850, p. 176.
9   For some account of the Rev. Dr George Mackay see *Biographies of Highland Clergymen* (Inverness, 1889), pp. 101-113.
10 General Assembly of the Free Church of Scotland Proposed translation of Dr Mackay. Proceedings of the Free Church of Scotland General Assembly 21 May 1853, pp. 44-45
11 SRO, CH. 3/146/37. Minutes of the Free Presbytery of Glasgow, 10 December 1867, pp. 378-381..

to which he was to minister for 25 years was composed almost entirely of Gaelic-speaking working class people, "domestic servants, apprentices, sailors and others in poor circumstances". Even so, because of his attractive ministry, Gordon enjoyed a good living. In the early years of his ministry the congregation achieved its greatest prosperity and in 1874 they were able to give their minister a supplement of £260.[12] In 1877 Evan Gordon received a call to Lawers which he declined to accept but by the 1880's Duke Street experienced a downturn in both attendances and income, unemployment apparently being a factor in the decline.[13] In 1881 Gordon visited America and in 1893 he retired to be succeeded by a Skye man, the Rev John Macleod. Gordon was said to be an active supporter of the Highland Land League. He died in 1904.

3.5   Hope Street Free Gaelic Church 1843-1900

In 1840 the managers of Hope Street Gaelic Church were concerned that the congregation's finances did not permit them to effect any reduction in the debt attaching to their building which, in accordance with normal practice, had been erected with borrowed money. However in the aftermath of the Disruption that liability worked to their advantage. In 1843 the congregation had, with one accord, followed their minister, the Rev. Walter MacGilvray, into the Free Church. Their building, of course, was the property of the Established Church but that church was now left without a congregation and therefore had no source of revenue with which to meet the interest payments due to the bondholders. The lenders, in order to recover their investment, forced a sale of the property — probably, as happened in other places, in collusion with the congregation's office-bearers. The Established Church was in no position to

12   Minutes of Duke Street Free Gaelic Church Deacons' Court, 15 May 1876.
13   *Ibid.*, 23 February 1880.

buy out the bondholders — it already had more buildings than congregations — and so 'friends' of the congregation purchased it on behalf of Hope Street Free Gaelic Church which eventually repaid the debt. In effect, this move simply transferred the debt from one creditor to another but it also severed any right which the Established Church had to the building, a stratagem employed to similar effect by many other congregations. In the absence of a debt, the congregation would have been deprived of their building (as happened in Duke St.) but Hope Street congregation entered the Free Church in circumstances virtually unchanged from those it enjoyed prior to 1843.

Walter MacGilvray as minister of Hope Street did not enjoy much rapport with his congregation. In 1845 the managers drew attention to the need to bring in a popular preacher for occasional weekday services with a view to improving their funds.[14] The minister was also advised that the supplement which he was paid (in addition to the Equal Dividend of £122) would be reduced from £200 to £120. Perhaps all of these circumstances served to encourage Walter MacGilvray to accept an invitation from the Colonial Committee to be seconded for work in Canada. Hope Street opposed both his decision to go for six months and his decision to extend his stay to twelve months but when, at the end of that time, he received a call to Vankleehill, Glengarry, Canada, the congregation did not object to his accepting the call. Although inducted to the charge of Vankleehill he stayed only one more year in Canada before returning in 1848 to Free St Mark's, Glasgow, the congregation that he had left in 1842 for Hope Street. His last charge, to which he moved in 1854, was Gilcomston Free Church (now Gilcomston South) Aberdeen. Like most vacant congregations when presented with the opportunity to select a minister the people of Hope Street initially set their sights on heavyweights and high-fliers such as

14   SRO, CH. 16/3/1/2, Minutes of Hope Street Free Gaelic Managers' Meeting, 25 April 1845.

Macrae, Knockbain (MacRath Mòr), who declined, choosing instead to go to Greenock Free Gaelic Church, or their former minister Alex Beith now of Stirling who also declined. Eventually they settled for a 24-year old probationer named Robert MacGillivray. Prior to his induction to Hope Street the congregation "had dwindled down to a mere handful"[15] and the task of rebuilding it proved too much for the young man whose health was such in 1852 that he was "advised not preach this winter but to pass the time at Bute".[16] The following year he accepted a call to Ballachulish where he died in 1865 aged 41.

Duncan MacGregor, the Loch-Tayside man who succeeded him, had also been born in 1824. His energy knew no bounds and in a short space of time he revitalised Hope Street. In the words of the Rev. Norman C. Macfarlane who wrote a fine sketch of his life, "he was an ideal pastor who yearned over the souls of his people".[17] Called from Stornoway Free Church to Hope Street in 1854 he gave ten years of ministry there and during that time he not only brought new life into that congregation but also applied his energies to the work of church extension to such effect that he built and established another church which, being a Gaelic congregation (the MacDonald Memorial) will receive more detailed notice later. MacGregor's ministry in Hope St. encompassed the years of the Second Evangelical Awakening and he himself testified that during these years "especially in 1859 and 1860, hardly a week passed, and often hardly a day but some one came to me with the cry of the three thousand, 'What shall we do?' (Acts 2 v. 37). It was a Pentecostal time"[18]

In 1864 MacGregor accepted a call to St Peter's Free Church, Dundee. This was the church of the saintly Robert

15 SRO, CH. 16/3/3/1, Minutes of Hope Street Free Gaelic Deacons' Court, 12 March 1849, p. 61.
16 *Ibid.*, 4 October 1852, p. 134.
17 Norman C. Macfarlane, *Apostles of the North. Sketches of some Highland Ministers* (Stornoway, ND), pp. 136-154.
18 Duncan MacGregor, *Memorial of Sabbath Evenings in Hope Street Church* (Glasgow, 1864), p. 2.

Murray McCheyne — a church which had been secured for the Free Church in 1843 by the same means (a forced sale to repay the bondholder) as had secured Hope Street. The church had become vacant through the appointment of the Rev. Islay Burns to a Chair in Trinity College and the McCheyne pulpit with all its hallowed associations had the same irresistible appeal for Duncan MacGregor as the Ferintosh pulpit had for his brother Malcolm.In Dundee he pursued his passion for church extension and built on the Perth Road the McCheyne Memorial Church which he got C. H. Spurgeon to open in 1870. Like St Peter's it remains open to this day. It was during his Dundee ministry that Duncan MacGregor wrote the brief account of his mother's cousin from Loch-Tayside, *Campbell of Kiltearn* — a delightful book which perpetuates the memory of one of the choicest pastors of the Highland church and of many of his ministerial contemporaries in the days of the fathers in Ross-shire [19]

To fill the vacancy consequent to MacGregor's translation to Dundee the Hope Street congregation followed the general practice of inviting the most celebrated ministers; but their optimism proved to be fruitless. They were no more persuasive with Dr Kennedy of Dingwall than was any other congregation and most seemed to have called him. Nor did they make any progress with Dr Aird of Creich. Eventually the seriously-divided congregation narrowly voted for Alex Urquhart of Tarbat in Easter Ross. The Presbytery refused to sustain the call initially but eventually agreed after it had been signed by 427 members and 386 adherents. Urquhart, who was a native of the Black Isle, gave faithful service from 1865 until his death in 1886 but on his appointment about half of the Hope Street office-bearers resigned their membership[20]. His obituarist described him as a solid preacher, the adjective being the

19 Duncan MacGregor, *Campbell of Kiltearn* (Edinburgh, 1874).
20 SRO, CH. 16/3/2/2, Hope Street Free Gaelic Kirk Session Minutes, 23 October 1865

accepted euphemism for dull. At the time of his death there were 526 names on the Communion Roll. During his ministry the congregation experienced most of the troubles that such a body can be heir to; the precentor was sacked on account of his singing, the tenant of the congregation's revenue-producing commercial property defaulted on payment of his rent owing to the depression in trade, the Sunday School children were reported as being very unruly and from time to time a like mutinous and unbrotherly behaviour was evident among the office-bearers. Even so, Alex Urquhart managed to keep the congregation in good heart and at regular intervals his Deacons' Court "on account of the congregation's prosperity" awarded him sums of £50 additional to his agreed supplement of £300 per annum.

The congregation took three years to fill the vacancy occasioned by the death of Alex Urquhart. Dr Kennedy's successor, Macaskill of Dingwall declined to be nominated as did John Noble of Lairg. The vacancy committee recommended Angus Galbraith of Raasay but the congregation voted for Ewan Macleod of Duthil despite averments that his enunciation was indistinct, his vocal range weak and his voice distinguished by "an extraordinary twang, all of which disqualify him to be an acceptable minister of the large and flourishing congregation of Hope Street Free Gaelic Church"[21]. Perhaps not surprisingly Macleod declined as later did Galbraith who as a student had attended Hope Street where he had relished the ministry of Duncan MacGregor.[22] Finally, the congregation elected James D MacCulloch of Latheron who was inducted in April 1889. It proved to be a particularly happy choice for Hope Street which he served with great acceptance for over 30 years — the longest ministry in its history.

21　SRO, CH. 16/3/2/3, Ibid., 28 February 1887, p. 132

22　For an account of the Rev. Angus Galbraith see Biographical Sketch prefacing *Sermons* (ed.by J. J. Galbraith, Inverness 1914).

It was during the vacancy following the death of Alex Urquhart that the church situated at the corner of Hope Street and Melville Street was sold. Realizing the capital value of the prime commercial site occupied by the Hope Street church had been a matter of discussion for 20 years previous to its sale in 1888 to the Standard Life Assurance Co. for £32,500. Ewing Place Congregational Church situated on Waterloo Street at West Campbell Street, which had been vacated following the Westward migration of that congregation to Hillhead, was purchased with one quarter of the sum realised from the Hope Street site, and the congregation, retaining its old name, resumed its life and witness in close proximity to its starting point. Migration to the affluent avenues of the West End was not an option for a Gaelic congregation.

3.6   Argyle Free Gaelic Church 1843-1900

On the brink of the Disruption the Established Presbytery of Glasgow agreed that an Argyllshire man, the Rev. Arch. MacDougall of Tarbert, Lochfyne, should be inducted to the newly formed dissentient Gaelic congregation which was meeting in the vacated Kirkfield Church on Buchan Street on the South side of the river. The Disruption then intervened and brought the entire congregation and its prospective minister out on the side of the Free Church. On 28 June 1843 the Free Presbytery of Glasgow gave its blessing to the proposal and MacDougall was inducted as minister of "the Gaelic congregation at present in Kirkfield". To begin with he was referred to as 'MacDougall of Kirkfield' and such was the shortage of Free Gaelic ministers in Glasgow in 1845 that the Presbytery refused to translate him when he was called to Balquhidder (Lochearnhead) or even when he was called to Kenmore where the very influential Marquis of Breadalbane was an elder.

In 1846 the Argyle congregation purchased a site in Oswald Street on the North side of the river and a new church costing £4400 and named after the Protestant martyr the Marquis of Argyle (beheaded in Edinburgh 1661) was opened in 1847.[23] The debt on the building when it opened was £2400 and it was finally cleared in 1869 largely through the exertions of the Rev Archibald MacDougall. When a special scheme to liquidate the debt was launched in 1860 the Deacons' Court agreed that £250 would be raised by the congregation (which consisted largely of working class people) and a further £250 would be raised by the minister from among his friends. In the event, the former group raised £500 and the latter £288.[24] In 1868 the minister was asked to raise £150 among his friends and he brought in £186; the Deacons' Court undertook to raise £80 "among friends not connected with the congregation" and £40 was to be raised by a Special Collection but only £11 was contributed. However the debt was finally cleared and in 1872 the congregation then applied itself to the purchase of a manse claiming it to be "the first manse ever provided for a Gaelic church in the city of Glasgow".[25] By 1874 MacDougall was aged 71 and he decided it was time to retire. Although the congregation during his pastorate had its share of squabbles, especially between the minister and office-bearers, generally speaking his ministry was a popular one. His preaching was said to be one of those instances "in which the manner is probably as effective as the matter".[26] He had an earnest and animated delivery — a style which always appealed to Highland hearts. However it was during their early days on the South side of the river and at the time of the revival in Ireland that both minister and people enjoyed the greatest blessing.[27]

23 SRO, CH. 3/1298/1, Statement on the origin of Argyle Church recorded in Argyle Church Deacons' Court Minutes, 6 February 1872. See also minute of 25 February 1869.

24 *Ibid.*, 17 January 1860.

25 *Ibid.*, 6 February 1872.

26 For an account of the Rev. Archibald MacDougall see John Smith, *Our Scottish Clergy* (Edinburgh, 1849), 2nd series, pp. 398-400.

27 SRO, CH. 3/1298/3. Tribute to the Rev. A MacDougall recorded in Argyle Church Kirk Session Minutes, 6 June 1883.

MacDougall was followed by another Argyllshire man, George L. Campbell, a native of Port Bannatyne, who had been minister for ten years in Lochs prior to his translation to Argyle. If MacDougall's relations with his office-bearers were, on occasion, stormy, with Campbell it was almost continuously so. Four men appointed successively as Session Clerk resigned between 1875 and 1881 and the fifth appointee died by drowning. Then the friction between minister and Deacons' Court reached such a pitch that in 1881 a group split off to form the West Campbell Street Mission. That same year on an appeal to the General Assembly by a group of office-bearers George L Campbell was warned against a lack of prudence in his financial dealings "which not unnaturally awakened a painful suspicion in the minds of members of the Deacons' Court as to the perfect straightforwardness of Mr Campbell in his intromissions with them".[28] However if that was bad, worse was to follow and in 1884 the Assembly suspended him on a charge of immorality. Subsequently he was employed by the Highlands and Islands Committee and in 1895 he settled in Shawbost ministering to that congregation for a number of years prior to his death in 1911. His ministry in Lochs (1865-75) was characterised as being a tirade against the Union negotiations[29] but in 1900 he entered the United Free Church as minister in Shawbost.

The Rev. Wm. Fraser, a native of Stratherrick, was translated to Argyle from Rothesay Chapelhill in 1884 and remained there until his retirement in 1906. He moved to Argyle at a time when the inclusion of hymns in congregational praise came to be seen as the touchstone of a congregation's relevance to the Church's mission to the world. When pressed to use hymns Fraser, "anxious to avoid anything that might tend to create

28 See *The Argyle Church Case* in the Proceedings of the Free Church of Scotland General Assembly 1881, pp 247-248.
29 Norman C Macfarlane, *Life of Donald J. Martin* (Edinburgh, 1914) p. 65.

dispeace in the congregation asked the Kirk Session to express their views freely and to come to some finding as to whether hymns should be sung at the Bible Class on Sunday evenings in the church". The Kirk Session, on the grounds that the Bible Class was not a regular service but the senior branch of the congregational Sunday School, approved of "a judicious use of hymns along with the Psalms at the Bible Class", the implementation of this policy to be at the discretion of the minister.[30] In 1893 the Oswald Street church was vacated and the Argyle congregation again crossed the river to the South side where they purchased the Gorbals Free Church located at the junction of King Street and Commerce Street. It now took the name Tradeston Gaelic Church and had a further eighteen years of life still to run as a separate congregation.

30   SRO, CH. 3/1298/3, Argyle Church Kirk Session Minutes, 23 December 1884.

4   GAELIC CHURCHES AND MISSIONS FORMED BETWEEN 1843 AND 1900

4.1   The Post-Disruption Gaelic Scene

The genesis of Duke Street (1798), Kirkfield (1813), Hope Street (1824) and Argyle (1842) Gaelic congregations was a consequence of a spontaneous generation arising out of communal enthusiasm. This spontaneity of action on the part of the Gaelic worshippers seems largely to have disappeared with the Disruption. Prior to the Disruption a Gaelic congregation could justify a claim for special treatment on language grounds and this encouraged the formation of new Gaelic groupings when corresponding English initiatives were liable to be suppressed as the intrigues of contrary dissenters. However the advantage that the Highlanders enjoyed over non-Gaelic groups disappeared after 1843 and the energies released by the Disruption seem to have been directed towards the establishment of English-speaking congregations. This may have been one factor contributing to the reduced activity on the Gaelic scene. Another, and more determinative factor was that by the middle of the 19th century most city-dwelling Gaelic speakers were bilingual and content to be associated with English congregations especially when this link identified them with a more elevated social status. The success of the Barony Church under Norman Macleod, eldest (but non-Gaelic-speaking) son of Norman Macleod of St Columba's Gaelic Church, was based at least partly on the Celtic appeal Norman of the Barony had for the Highlander.

The Disruption gave rise to a tremendous enthusiasm for church multiplication. The classic example is that of the Wynd Free Church which in a few years divided into four congregations and ultimately, through its daughter churches, claimed to have founded no fewer than 23 congregations.[1] But this vitality was not shared by the Gaelic congregations. These congregations had too high a proportion of migrant worshippers to allow them develop the dynamism of the emergent middle-class English congregations. The result was that in contrast to the earlier part of the 19th century when lay initiative brought new Gaelic congregations such as Duke Street and Hope Street into being, the middle decades of the century witnessed the abdication of grassroots leadership in Gaelic church extension in favour of stipendiary leadership from Presbytery and Assembly committees. Additionally there was some local initiative associated with individually-concerned ministers, congregational rivalry, and disaffected office-bearers.

4.2   The Glasgow Home Highland Mission

As early as 1844 the Free Church Assembly appointed a Gaelic Committee to assist the establishment of weak congregations. In 1845 it became a part of the Home Mission Committee but it was again disjoined in 1849, this time as the Highland Committee, the name delineating the territorial limits of its remit while the Home Mission Committee was made responsible for the Lowlands. Even so the Highland Committee was responsible for promoting work among migrant Highlanders in the Lowlands and it pursued energetically that part of its remit. However there was a certain amount of overlap between the Highland Committee and home mission committees formed by the Free Presbytery of Glasgow. In 1851 the Free Assembly Home Mission Committee appointed a Committee for the Evangelization of Glasgow and this had some early success with English-speaking congregations. There was also a Free

---

1   Wm. Ewing, (ed.), *Annals of the Free Church of Scotland* (2 vols., Edinburgh, 1914), vol. 2, p. 104. For an account of this remarkable expansion see D. MacColl, *Work in the Wynds* (Glasgow, 1872).

Presbytery of Glasgow Committee on Highland Evangelization (1855) sometimes referred to as the Glasgow Home Highland Mission, the first secretary of which was the minister of Duke Street the Rev. George C Macleod. Ultimately this committee of Presbytery was discharged, probably because it never really succeeded in co-ordinating mission outreach to the Glasgow Highlanders. Its actual, if not its intended, role appeared to be largely that of mediating congregational rivalries but in 1855 with an estimated 45,000 Highlanders resident in Glasgow and only four Gaelic churches (one Established and three Free) there was no shortage of fallow ground and so the Free Assembly's Highland Committee encouraged the Free Presbytery of Glasgow's Home Highland Mission to prosecute the work with the assistance of funding from the Highland Committee. By 1861 the minister of Argyle Gaelic Church, the Rev. Archibald MacDougall, was urging the Highland Committee to allocate its financial support equally among the three Free Gaelic congregations.[2] This was surely an indication that each congregation wanted to go it alone in respect of outreach. It was a time when every self-respecting minister and congregation had to have a church extension project and so the Glasgow Home Highland Mission as a joint or coordinating committee was dissolved. Each of the Gaelic churches had its mission outreach but only one showed any prospect of success.

4.3   The MacDonald Memorial Gaelic Church, Cowcaddens

The first and most notable of the Gaelic Missions was that which came to be known as the MacDonald Memorial, a church founded by the Rev. Duncan MacGregor, minister of Hope

---

2   SRO, CH. 3/983/1, Minutes of the Free Church of Scotland Highlands and Islands Committee, 19 March 1861, p.308.

Street Free Church (1854-1864), in memory of the Rev. John MacDonald of Ferintosh. The Rev. Norman C. MacFarlane in his book *Apostles of the North* has a curious comment on MacGregor's Hope Street ministry. He wrote, "There were many estimable Highlanders in Hope Street Church but there were others. They shrank from and disliked evangelistic work. They curiously thought the devil was chief shareholder in it".[3] In Breadalbane MacGregor had been reared in an atmosphere of evangelistic outreach. All his instincts lay in that direction and in 1859 when revival broke out in Ireland he crossed the channel (as did his colleague Arch. MacDougall, minister of Argyle Gaelic Church) to see and to share in that work. He returned to Glasgow fully determined to launch out into church extension. According to Macfarlane his position was not comfortable for "many of the old-fashioned Highlanders rejected at his views". But in June 1860 he asked for and obtained the support of his Kirk Session. An extract from the Kirk Session minute book reads, "The Kirk Session of Hope Street congregation being deeply impressed with the spiritual wants of their countrymen in Glasgow, especially in Cowcaddens, Port Dundas and Townhead, have resolved to commence territorial operations among them and to apply to the Home Mission Committee for a grant to help them in said operations".

When MacGregor brought this resolution to the Presbytery for their necessary approval he "made a lengthened statement showing that a large proportion of the Highlanders in Glasgow were living in the neglect of ordinances and that the Territorial scheme was the only one which under the divine blessing promised to reclaim them to churchgoing habits".[4] The Presbytery thanked him for bringing the matter before them and, as if suddenly reminded that they had years ago appointed

---

3   Norman C. Macfarlane, *Apostles of the North, Sketches of some Highland Ministers* (Stornoway, ND), p. 147.
4   SRO, CH. 3/146/35, Minutes of the Free Presbytery of Glasgow, 6 June 1860, p. 302.

a committee to pursue this praiseworthy objective, they gave notice to the minister of Duke Street, as secretary of the Gaelic Home Mission Committee that they wanted a report of that committee's stewardship. Within a year the committee was dismissed but MacGregor's Cowcaddens project got official approval in September and by October 1861 a building was rising fast at 100 Maitland Street and a new Highland congregation was joyfully anticipated by the Assembly's Highland Committee.

A distinctive architectural feature of the new building was an external stone pulpit subtended midway up an outside wall with access to it through a door set in the side of the building. From this vantage point it would have been possible to harangue an audience in the street below but apparently this method of open-air preaching was discouraged by the municipal authority possibly as being provocative of Irish-Catholic sensitivities. The church was demolished in 1964.[5]

Agents, students and probationers had all been engaged in the pastoral groundwork but the committee were anxious to recruit a prominent preacher for the new station and they appointed Dr MacKintosh Mackay who had recently returned to Scotland from St George's, Sydney[6]. At first, Dr Mackay "reacted favourably, although not in writing". Later, however, he had second thoughts and the station continued to be supplied with probationers until the Rev. John Gordon was translated from Evanton in 1864. That same year the church's founder, MacGregor of Hope Street removed to Dundee where, in an action replay of the Cowcaddens church extension project, he established the McCheyne Memorial Church. The attitude of the Hope Street office-bearers towards the Cowcaddens Mission was at best less than wholehearted. When the Hope

5   *The City That Disappeared* (p. 92) by Frank Worsdall, (Glasgow 1981.)
6   For a biographical sketch of Dr Mackintosh Mackay written by Dr John Kennedy, see J. Graham (ed.) *Disruption Worthies of the Highlands. A Memorial of 1843.* (Edinburgh, 1886), enlarged edition pp. 79-88.

Street Kirk Session learned that the Cowcaddens project had been approved by the Highland Committee the Session were careful to minute "their willingness to continue their assistance in carrying on the work in the Cowcaddens station but owing to the heavy debt on their own church they felt constrained to keep themselves and their congregation free of any pecuniary responsibility in the matter"[7]. Duncan MacGregor, by his own endeavours, raised £3200 and the MacDonald Memorial Church was opened free of debt. This auspicious opening did not guarantee a successful operation. Within three years the office-bearers of the new church decided that the other side of the Clyde offered "a more eligible situation" and Presbytery was asked to sanction a move in that direction. In 1868 the minister, "amid declining health and a heavy domestic affliction and bereavement" accepted a call to Tobermory but before he got there he died aged 46.

In the ensuing vacancy the Presbytery proposed a union of MacDonald Church with Duke Street Gaelic which, since 1847, was located on Mains Street only half a mile distant from MacDonald Gaelic. Duke Street was vacant at the time and the Presbytery hoped to unite the two congregations in the Duke Street building and to use the MacDonald building to house an English-speaking Cowcaddens congregation.[8] Naturally, the Duke Street congregation had no objection to this proposal but the MacDonald congregation successfully resisted it and called the Rev John Logan, a firebrand from Duthil, as their minister[9]. He continued the pressure on Presbytery to move the congregation across the river to Plantation but he died within the space of three years and that brief ministry was followed by an equally brief one from the

---

7   SRO, CH. 16/3/2/1, Minutes of Hope Street Free Gaelic Kirk Session, 23 September 1861, p. 212.
8   SRO, CH. 3/146/35, Minutes of the Free Presbytery of Glasgow, 1 July 1868, p. 438.
9   For a description of the Rev. John Logan, see Donald Maclean, *Duthil: Past and Present* (Inverness, 1910), pp. 50-64.

Rev. Angus MacIver, a native of Ross-shire, whose personal qualities have received unflattering treatment from the pitiless pen of N C Macfarlane.[10] In 1875 MacIver transferred to the Church of Scotland and was admitted to Uig but he rejoined the Free Church being listed as a Probationer in 1900. He was inducted as Free Church minister in Strathconon in 1907 and died in 1915.

On the appointment of the Rev. Alex Murchison from Helmsdale in 1876 the congregation was at long last raised to the Equal Dividend Platform. Murchison led his people into the union of 1900 and on his retirement in 1902 the congregation ceased to be a Gaelic charge. That same year, re-sanctioned as an English charge, it was renamed Phoenix Park but the building closed in 1907 when Phoenix Park was united with Somerville Memorial. Somerville, in turn, was linked with Cowlairs in 1965 and, as Cowlairs-Somerville, linked ultimately with Springburn North and Springburn Hill as Springburn.[11]

The outworking of Duncan MacGregor's vision of a Gaelic Mission in Cowcaddens failed to live up to his expectations. In the middle of last century the main Sunday service tended to be the afternoon service, the morning service being less well attended. MacDonald Memorial began with English in the morning and Gaelic in the afternoon but as early as 1865 the Presbytery was asked to reverse this arrangement and make the popular diet an English service. Then, in 1868, the Presbytery sought to suppress MacDonald Memorial as a Gaelic Charge on the grounds that the original representations as to the number of Gaelic-speaking people desirous of having Gospel ordinances in Gaelic were not justified by subsequent events. Many of the people who attached themselves to MacDonald Memorial were entirely unacquainted with Gaelic and the Gaelic usage in the church was so limited as to take

---

10 Norman C. Macfarlane, *Life of Rev. Donald J. Martin* (Edinburgh, 1914), p. 65.
11 *Fasti Ecclesiae Scoticanae* vol. 10 (Edinburgh, 1981).

from it the character of a Gaelic charge. Having that reputation it was bypassed by Gaelic devotees.

4.4   Cowcaddens Free Church

At the same time as MacGregor of Hope Street began his
Cowcaddens Gaelic Mission, Dr Walter Smith of the Free Tron
Church also began a mission work in that area. This was the
group to which the Presbytery purposed to transfer the
MacDonald church in 1868. When that plan failed the
Cowcaddens Free Church was erected in 1872 on Maitland
Street just down the road from the MacDonald church. It too
was very much a working class congregation and in 1882 its
second pastorate commenced under the Rev. William Ross, a
Gaelic speaker from Caithness whose previous charge had been
in Rothesay. Ross was not just a Gaelic speaker, he was a Gaelic
scholar and when the first appointment was made to the Celtic
Chair in the University of Edinburgh he ran a close second to
Professor Wm. Watson.[12]   By the time that Ross went to
Cowcaddens Free Church it had become greatly weakened but
under Ross's aggressive evangelism it revived. Ross used every
possible means of promoting it including occasional Gaelic
services and even Gaelic communions. The effect of this, of
course, was to further undermine the Gaelic strength of the
MacDonald Memorial. Cowcaddens Free Church entered the
Union of 1900 becoming Cowcaddens United Free and, as
Cowcaddens Church of Scotland, was terminated in 1967 when it
was united with St Stephens, Blythswood. It is now part of Renfield
St Stephen's, a grouping of at least eleven former congregations.

4.5   St Columba's Free Gaelic, Govan

A Free Gaelic congregation in Govan had its beginning in a
petition addressed to the Free Assembly's Highland Committee

12   J. M. E. Ross, *William Ross of Cowcaddens. A Memoir* (London, 1905), pp. 83-84. See
     also John J. Rae, *The Ministers of Glasgow* (Glasgow, ND), pp. 225-233.

in March 1862.[13] In April a meeting was held in Govan Free Church to consider the special needs of Highlanders and it was resolved at that meeting that the only solution was a Gaelic Territorial church, i.e., a church specifically for that area[14]. The Returns for 1863 indicated that there were over 700 Gaelic-speaking parishioners in Govan but, even so, the Highland Committee had some doubts regarding the extent of popular demand for Gaelic services and these doubts were shared by the Presbytery. As it happened, a mere two years later, the Rev. Gilbert Johnston, the minister of Govan Free Church, defected to the Church of Scotland and the petition for a Gaelic charge may have represented Highland conservative dissatisfaction with the incumbent. The Presbytery did not want to erect a new Gaelic preaching station and felt the need could be met by the appointment of a probationer who would "hold two diets of worship every Sabbath one of them during the day in Gaelic to be held in a room or hall rented by the people themselves and the other in the other language to be held in Govan Free Church freely granted for the purpose by Mr Johnston". This arrangement it was said, "does essentially provide for the Highlanders in Govan to the extent, if not precisely in the form, in which they sought it"[15]. This may well have been a coded statement implying that the Highlanders simply wanted another preacher in English or in Gaelic.

In 1863 a petition in favour of the appointment of the Rev. A. C. Fullarton (a native of Arran and highly rated as a Gaelic preacher) was signed by 406 Highlanders of Govan. Fullarton had given two months supply but it seems he did not agree to a lengthier appointment. In July 1865 the Govan Highlanders asked the Highland Committee to secure for them the services of Murdo Macaskill, a Lewisman who eventually became successor to Dr Kennedy of Dingwall but who at the

---

13   SRO, CH. 3/983/1, Minutes of the Highland Committee, 15 March 1862, p. 345.
14   SRO, CH. 3/146/36, Minutes of the Free Presbytery of Glasgow, 7 May 1862, p. 462.
15   Ibid., 6 May 1863, p. 540.

time was a divinity student acting as Gaelic missioner at Partick. In his diary entry Macaskill[16] expressed his misgivings as to his suitability for this responsible post with "its solemn duties" but little of this was evident in his negotiations with the Govan congregation or with the Highland Committee, the practical import of which was that he could be induced to leave Partick for Govan if it was made worth his while; and it was.[17] After his first year in Govan, Macaskill decided that the popular evening service should be in English every Sunday instead of alternating with Gaelic every second Sunday and that laymen could hold district meetings in Gaelic on a Sunday evening for those who preferred Gaelic. Macaskill's ministry was popular and the opening services of a new church were held in September 1867. The congregation hoped to retain Macaskill when he had completed his divinity course but as Govan Gaelic was only a mission station and not a sanctioned charge its ministerial emoluments stood at a lower level and in 1868 Macaskill accepted a call to Glenlyon.

In 1870 the Presbytery consulted the congregation about a possible union with the MacDonald Gaelic Church but nothing came of that and in 1874 Govan Free Gaelic was made a sanctioned charge. The original building was now replaced with a new church located on Winsor Street. The new building named St Columba Free Church, Govan, was opened in 1877. In 1878 the congregation claimed to be doing the work of an English Territorial charge having three English services every Sunday. The wants of the Gaelic-speaking population of Govan seemed to be satisfied with kitchen meetings but the congregation did attempt to do Gaelic outreach work in Plantation and Kinning Park where in 1876 it was said there were at least 3000 Gaelic speakers. These people were located about one

16 Biographical sketch by John Macaskill prefacing *A Highland Pulpit* Being Sermons of the Late Rev. Murdoch Macaskill (Inverness, 1907), p. vi.
17   SRO, CH. 3/645/5. Minute Book of the Highland Mission Govan (Free St Columba, Govan), 27 July 1865.

and a half miles from any Gaelic church and St Columba's (the only Free Gaelic church South of the river), in seeking funding from the Highland Committee, claimed that their method of evangelising these Highlanders would not put pressure on them to join the Govan Church but would leave them free to choose their congregation.[18]   In 1889 the congregation were still operating a Plantation mission in a hall which they rented from Paisley Road Free Church.

The first minister to be inducted to the charge sanctioned in 1874 was the Rev. Allan Cameron. Ordained to St Columba's in 1874 he moved to Ardrossan in 1887 and to the East Church Inverness in 1892.[19] He died in 1928. He was succeeded in St Columba's by the Rev. John T. Maclean who retired in 1899 and he, in turn, was succeeded by a Glen Urquhart man, the Rev. Evan Grant.[20]

4.6   St Kiaran's Gaelic Church of Scotland, Govan

Concern for the provision of Gaelic services in Glasgow was not confined to the Free Church. The sixties of last century was a period of remarkable recovery and expansion in the Church of Scotland and no better illustration of this is to be found than the parish of Govan. At that time the population on the South side of the river was expanding rapidly. Between 1836 and 1876 it increased fivefold to approximately 220,000.[21] When Matthew Leishman went to Govan in 1821 it was "an average country cure".[22] When he died in 1874 it was "the richest living in the Church of Scotland". He is credited with having built 12 chapels in Govan so that Govan bore more

---

18 SRO, CH. 3/983/3, Minutes of the Highland Committee, 19 December 1876, p. 89.

19 J. A. Lamb (ed.) *The Fasti of the United Free Church of Scotland* (Edinburgh, 1956) p. 473

20 *Ibid.*, p. 223.

21 A. C. Drummond and J. Bulloch, *The Church in Late Victorian Scotland 1874-1900* (Edinburgh, 1978), p. 204.

22 James F. Leishman, *Matthew Leishman of Govan* (Paisley, 1921), pp. 209-210.

resemblance to a diocese than to a Parish.[23] Yet it is not to Govan Parish Church but to the office-bearers of Glasgow's first Gaelic Church that credit is due for commencing a Gaelic congregation under the auspices of the Established Church in Govan.

In 1866 "a neat little church was secured" on Burndyke Street near the South bank of the Clyde. Known as Govan Highland Church or Govan Gaelic Chapel, it was a Highland mission under the care of St Columba's Hope Street and supported by the Home Mission Committee of the Church of Scotland. From 1866 the congregation had a succession of temporary and not always satisfactory preachers and no lengthy ministry was established until the appointment in 1879 of the Rev. Duncan MacNair Connell, an Argyllshire man of some-what explosive temperament who negotiated with the vacancy committee of Govan Gaelic while still Free Church minister of Fortingall.[24] He was elected unanimously and after 17 years in Fortingall he went to Govan, his second and last charge. His relationship with his office-bearers was somewhat stormy and he found himself at the receiving end of the kind of treatment to which as a student and schoolteacher in Aberdeen he had subjected the hapless minister of the Aberdeen Gaelic Chapel.[25] Perhaps his main claim to fame is as author of the only book on astronomy ever to be written in Gaelic.[26]

In 1884 the church was made a *quoad sacra* parish with the name St Kiaran's. It continued to have a succession of Gaelic-speaking ministers the last being the Rev. John McKechnie, subsequently Reader in Celtic in the University of Aberdeen and the author of several Gaelic books perhaps the best known being *Gaelic Without Groans*. When he left in 1931

23 A. Wallace, *The Parish of Govan As It Was and As It Is* (Glasgow, 1877), p. 177.

24 SRO, CH. 2/1023/3, Govan Gaelic Chapel Managers' Minutes, 28 April 1879.

25 Aberdeen Gaelic Chapel Managers' Minutes.

26 D. M. Connell, *Reul-eolas. Gaelic Astronomy* (Edinburgh, ND). For a description of D. M. Connell, see Alex Stewart, *A Highland Parish* (Glasgow, 1928), p. 224; also obituary notice in *Govan Press* of 23 June 1905.

the church was vacated and the congregation linked with Dean's Park but provision was made in the Basis of Union for Gaelic-speaking members of St Kiaran's to transfer to St Columba-Copland Road which was the continuation of the former Govan Free Church. Both sections of St Kiaran's were to come together again with the merger in 1976 of St Columba's-Summertown with St Kiaran's-Deans Park as Govan Trinity, now part of New Govan. As a Gaelic congregation the attendances in St Kiaran's never came up to expectations and, in an attempt to make the congregation more viable, consideration was given to holding two English series each Sunday as early as 1882.[27]

4.7   Partick Free Gaelic Church

In 1843 Partick was a village of some 2000 inhabitants but thereafter it grew very rapidly reaching 35,000 in 1876.[28] By the end of the Rev. Henry Anderson's fifty-year pastorate, Anderson Free Church which he had built in green fields, found itself in the midst of slums. This expansion was sustained by substantial immigration of Highlanders and as early as 1864 Henry Anderson had the divinity student Murdo Macaskill doing mission work among the Gaelic speakers of Partick before he was enticed to Govan. Anderson Free Church supported a great deal of mission work in the Partick area, much of it carried on by Gaelic-speaking divinity students.[29] In 1873 a petition came to the Free Assembly's Highland Committee from eighteen members and adherents of Partick stating that of the 250 Highlanders in the Burgh, 100 did not attend any place of worship.[30] The petition, requesting funds to support a Gaelic

27 A. C. Drummond and J. Bulloch, *The Church in Late Victorian Scotland 1874-1900* (Edinburgh, 1978), p . 204.
28 H. Anderson, *Reminiscences of a Pastorate of Fifty Years* (Glasgow, 1896), p. 32.
29 SRO, CH. 3/983/2, Minutes of the Highland Committee, 21 January 1873, p. 319.
30 SRO, CH. 3/983/4, Minutes of the Highland Committee, 22 March 1887, p. 80.

missionary, was granted to the extent of £5 for a student missionary. A Gaelic mission was commenced and the next year support for a permanent missionary in place of students was requested and a £10 annual grant was awarded but it was increased to £20 in 1875 so that a catechist could be employed. In 1876 it was reported that the mission was flourishing and as the people were contributing £40 to the missionary, the Committee's grant was increased to £30. In 1879 the Presbytery raised the mission to the status of a regular station. The Rev. G.D.R. Munro of Jordanhill Free Church acted as Interim-Moderator and the Highland Committee appointed the Rev. G.G. Macleod as preacher. This was the George Macleod who had been active as secretary of the Glasgow Gaelic Mission from 1855 when he was minister of Duke Street. However in 1868 he had resigned from Duke Street after the Presbytery had commenced disciplinary proceedings against him because of his reported alcoholism. After his resignation from Duke Street, the Highland Committee employed him from time to time on various assignments and he continued in Partick as the agent of the Highland Committee until 1882 when the local managing committee requested his removal. A series of divinity students, among them Peter MacDonald later minister in Stornoway, now supplied the station until the General Assembly of 1887, acting on the advice of the Presbytery, raised Partick Gaelic Mission to a full ministerial charge, Evan Gordon minister of Duke Street alone dissenting.[31] The first minister elected to the charge was the Rev. Alex Macrae. Ordained and inducted to Partick in 1898 he and his congregation entered the Union of 1900 and shortly afterwards Macrae moved to Creich where he made his contribution to the literature of the Highlanders with his *Revivals in the Highlands (1905)* and *The Life of Dr Aird (1908)*.

31   SRO, CH. 3/983/4, Minutes of the Highland Committee, 22 March 1887, p. 80.

4.8   Gaelic Mission Stations

In addition to the Gaelic mission stations which were eventually elevated to the status of Gaelic charges there were a number of Gaelic missions that failed to become established.

4.8.1 Broomielaw Gaelic Mission

In 1863 the Argyle congregation under the Rev. Archibald MacDougall sought funding from the Highland Committee to support outreach to non-churchgoing Highlanders at Broomielaw. This work was carried on spasmodically at least until 1886 despite opposition from the minister of Hope Street who moved in Presbytery that "the grant to Argyle Church be withdrawn on the ground that the district is occupied by another missionary and that the work for which said grant was given has not been done inasmuch as the missionary was employed to do congregational work instead of territorial work".[32] On the face of it the objection raised by the Rev. Alex Urquhart has the appearance of congregational rivalry but it is more likely that it was prompted by concern over the Argyle minister's (G. L. Campbell) imprudent handling of finances.

4.8.2. Maryhill Gaelic Mission

In 1871 the Highland Committee in response to an appeal from the Free Presbytery of Glasgow agreed to employ a student to work among Gaelic-speaking navvies at Maryhill and John Mackay, who in later years proved to be one of the church's most successful Highland evangelists, was recruited to this work as a student.[33] In 1872 a student probationer — Alex Cameron

---

32   SRO, CH. 3/983/3, Minutes of the Highland Committee, 18 May 1881, p. 262.
33   A. Mackenzie, *The Rev. John Mackay, Student, Pastor, Highland Evangelist* (Paisley, 1921), p. 35.

— who had the backing of the Duke Street minister, was employed with some reluctance by the Highland Committee to work with non-churchgoing Highlanders in Maryhill.[34] A year later the committee deferred renewing the grant "until evidence be produced that the other half of Mr Cameron's salary will be secured as hinted by him" At this point Hope Street stepped in to support the probationer who at one time had been attached to that congregation, serving briefly as its Session Clerk. Alex Cameron failed to sustain the confidence of Free Church circles and when he asked the committee for an appointment in the Highlands he was told they would be agreeable if any should ask for him but none did. However he found more of a welcome in the Church of Scotland and was much lamented by the people of Reay when he died in 1896 after serving 20 years in the Sherrey Mission.[35] By 1875 the missionary employed by the Highland Committee reported that "the Highlanders were fast leaving Maryhill for other places where they could get work" and the committee then decided to discontinue the mission.[36] The Highlanders that remained seemingly transferred their support to the Partick Gaelic Mission but it is possible that some moved in the other direction to Springburn.

4.8.3 Springburn Gaelic Mission

In July 1875 the Highland Committee received a letter from a James Mackenzie employed by Messrs Nelson & Co., Hyde Park Locoworks, Springburn. He wrote to say that for four years he had been holding Gaelic services in his home at which divinity students officiated but now his employers were willing to grant the free use of their hall on Sabbath evenings for a

---

34 SRO, CH. 3/983/2, Minutes of the Highland Committee, 22 October 1872, p. 306.
35 John O'Groat Journal Friday 28 February 1896. For an account of the Rev.Alex Cameron, see D. Mackay, *Memories of Our Parish* (Dingwall, 1925), pp. 85-90.
36 SRO, CH. 3/983/3, Minutes of the Highland Committee, 20 April 1875, p. 7.

Gaelic meeting if it would be regularly maintained. Mackenzie said there were thirty families interested and he requested the committee to appoint and support a probationer — Alex Cameron — for this work.[37] The Committee agreed to a grant of £20. The following April Mackenzie appeared before the Hope Street Kirk Session with a petition signed by 195 Gaelic-speaking persons styling themselves Springburn Gaelic Mission requesting official superintendence by the Hope Street Kirk Session. Hope Street appointed a committee to watch over them and the Highlanders renewed their application to the Highland Committee and requested that Alex Cameron be replaced by a Lewisman whom they named. The choice of preacher was apparently made by the local committee and did not please the people who sent a deputation to make known their displeasure. The mission was supplied by divinity students until 1885 when the local committee requested the services of the Rev. G. G. Macleod, the former minister of Duke Street who had until recently been supplying the Partick Gaelic Mission. Probably on account of the ill health of the minister of Hope Street (Alex Urquhart who died in 1886) the Highland Committee, on the recommendation of the Presbytery, transferred the superintendence of the Springburn Mission to Cowcaddens Free Church and its Gaelic-speaking minister, William Ross. George G. Macleod continued in Springburn until 1888 when he asked for "an appointment to a station in the country on account of the state of his health" but none was available and he died that same year.[38]

In 1891 a petition signed by 231 persons belonging to the Springburn mission requested that Hope Street, now under the Rev. J. D. MacCulloch, would again undertake superintendence of the mission and MacCulloch's concern to promote its welfare was soon apparent.[39] The mission committee

---

37 *Ibid.*, 20 July 1875, p. 22
38 SRO, CH. 3/983/4, Minutes of the Highland Committee, 17 April 1888, p. 109
39 SRO, CH. 16/3/2/3, Hope Street Free Gaelic Church Kirk Session Minutes, 20 May 1891, p.200..

obtained a feu at the North end of Coburg Place on which they proposed to erect an iron Mission Hall at a cost of £250.[40] MacCulloch, however, got the opportunity to buy for £60 an iron building which had been used as a school at Possilpark and which for another £70 he estimated could be removed and erected at Springburn. Acting on his own initiative he completed the deal and received the approval of his Deacons' Court. It seems however that the Highlanders showed insufficient interest in maintaining the mission for within a year the local Baptist minister, John Horn, was negotiating the purchase of the iron hall and in 1893 it was sold to the Baptists for £200.[41] This left the Gaelic Mission with the need to "look out and fix on a suitable place for holding meetings" and they settled on a shop in Keppochhill Road which they shared as mission premises with Sighthill Free Church. When in 1896 the Sighthill church had no further use for the shop, the Gaelic Mission retained it but in 1898 they were again approached by the Baptists "for the use of the Mission Hall on the days and evenings not occupied by the Gaelic Mission".[42] A sublet was agreed to. By 1904 the Baptists had built in Springburn a church costing £3800[43] whereas the Gaelic Mission was occupying rented premises on Springburn Road. In 1907 the Hope Street Deacons' Court "in view of the small numbers attending the meetings, agreed to give up that Mission"[44]. After thirty years of Gaelic Mission work there was no visible congregation in Springburn and continuance could no longer be justified.

40 SRO, CH. 16/3/3/3, Hope Street Free Gaelic Church Deacons' Court Minutes, 6 January 1892.
41 *Ibid.*, 5 October 1893.
42 *Ibid.*, 5 January 1898.
43 G. Yuille, *History of the Baptists in Scotland* (Glasgow, 1926) pp. 185-186.
44 SRO, CH. 16/3/2/3, Hope Street Free Gaelic Church Kirk Session Minutes, 26 February 1907.

4.8.4 Kinning Park and Plantation Gaelic Mission

On the basis of a survey of the distribution of Gaelic speakers in Glasgow in 1890, Hope Street Kirk Session selected four areas for Gaelic missionary outreach, viz., Anderston, Calton, Townhead and an unspecified fourth district which turned out to be Kinning Park and Plantation. Closer scrutiny, however, revealed that "the Gaelic-speaking people in the Calton and Townhead districts which the Session once thought suitable localities for carrying on missionary operations were not so numerous as to warrant an outlay of pecuniary means compared to other districts in the city".[45] Unexpectedly they discovered that there were a large number of Gaelic-speaking people in the Paisley Road district. At that time the better-off families were beginning to leave Kinning Park for more suburban areas and the Highlanders were among those now moving in. Other agencies also had an eye to this new mission field but Hope Street Kirk Session "resolved to open a mission for lapsed Highlanders in the Plantation and Kinning Park district and as far removed from the areas occupied by other Gaelic agencies as will be found compatible with usefulness". In June 1891 the Session received a petition from 123 Highlanders residing in Plantation asking for supervision but the Session was somewhat inhibited from acting on account of a Presbytery decision "to keep the district open for the Argyle congregation for one year". The Argyle congregation had in fact commenced operations on the South side of the river in 1890 and in 1893 they left Oswald Street for Tradeston and took the name Tradeston Gaelic. However the Hope Street session secured a hall in Plantation and maintained some desultory activity there for ten years. Another congregation active in Plantation was St Columba's Free Gaelic, Govan who, from the 1880's, were grant-aided for this work by the

45   Ibid., 26 November 1890, p. 192.

Highland Committee. This congregation's work enjoyed the particular favour of Principal Rainy, the convener of the Highland Committee, for in 1887 when grants were being reduced to all mission stations he undertook to find some additional support for St Columba's Plantation work and he made a similar offer in 1890.[46]

4.8.5 Clydebank Gaelic Mission

As the century progressed and the shipyards moved further down the river to Govan, Partick, Scotstown and Clydebank, the people moved with them. In 1890 the Presbyteries of Glasgow and Dunbarton proposed that Gaelic services should be held at Clydebank with responsibility being shared by Clydebank Hamilton Memorial Free Church and Partick Free Gaelic Church. In 1892 the Clydebank Free Church sought a renewal of the Highland Committee grant for their Gaelic Mission but the Committee had before them at the same time "a memorial from Highlanders connected with another Gaelic Mission at Clydebank objecting to the giving of the grant". The Committee deferred the application for further enquiry but eventually agreed to the renewal of the grant. [47]

4.8.6 West Campbell Street Mission

A serious split occurred in the Argyle congregation in late 1881. It was precipitated by suspicions entertained by the treasurer and several of the deacons concerning the integrity of the minister, the Rev. G.L. Campbell, in his handling of grants to the congregation from the Highland Committee. The Presbytery had exonerated the minister and the General Assembly upheld this decision when it was appealed against by the office-bearers.[48] But

46 SRO, CH. 3/983/4, Minutes of the Highland Committee, 20 March 1888, p. 104.
47 *Ibid.*, 16 February 1892, p. 236.
48 Proceedings of the Free Church of Scotland General Assembly 28 May 1881, pp. 247-248.

lack of confidence persisted and at the end of the year nine elders and nine deacons resigned and then withdrew to form the West Campbell Street Mission.[49] The Presbytery, making a virtue out of necessity, recognised the Mission on the understanding that it would be no burden to any of the funds of the Church and the Rev. John McNeill, a native of Tiree, was given charge of the Mission. When the Rev. G. L. Campbell was removed from Argyle in 1884 on a disciplinary charge and a new minister inducted, overtures were made to the rebels in West Campbell Street and they agreed to return on condition that they would be received on the same footing as that on which they had left, i.e., as elders, deacons or members of Argyle.[50] John McNeill left for Auldearn and so ended the short-lived West Campbell Street Mission.

49   SRO, CH. 3/1298/3, Argyle Free Gaelic Kirk Session Minutes, 26 December 1881, p. 218.
50   Ibid., 5 January 1885.

5   POST-1900 CHURCHES WITH GAELIC MINISTRY

5.1   The Union of the Churches in 1900 and 1929

In October 1900 the great majority of the ministers and congregations of the Free Church of Scotland entered into a union with the United Presbyterian Church to form the United Free Church of Scotland. This Union had first been proposed at an official level in 1863 but, in the face of strong opposition from the conservative wing of the church, these early union negotiations were discontinued in 1873 when it was felt that to continue threatened to split the church.[1] However, by 1894, the most redoubtable of the opposition leaders — James Begg of Newington and John Kennedy of Dingwall — were dead and union negotiations were resumed. The opposition was now largely confined to the Highland area and Principal Rainy, the Free Church leader of the Union movement, was hopeful that the Highland opponents of union would confine their disapproval to a formal protest which stopped short of the threatened split. In this he was disappointed. The conservative minority not only refused to enter the Union but claimed that those from the Free Church who did, were in breach of their ordination vows. They further asserted that since the action of the Unionists was contrary to the law of the church, the United Free Church had no entitlement to Free Church property. So confident were the minority of their ground that they took their case to the House of Lords which, in a historic decision delivered in 1904, found in favour of the appellants by a majority of five to two. In consequence of this decision, the minority were able to exercise their claim to be the continuing Free Church of Scotland.

Notwithstanding this decision, it was evident to both sides that the victors could not possibly use the buildings that were

---

1   J. H. S. Burleigh, *A Church History of Scotland* (Oxford, 1960), p. 364.

legally theirs for they had neither ministers nor congregations to occupy them. Consequently a Commission was appointed by Act of Parliament to allocate the churches' property between the contending parties. The basis of allocation was generally understood to be that a building was to be allocated to the Free Church where it could be established that one third of the members and adherents belonging to the congregation in 1900 were opposed to the Union. In the greater Glasgow area there were 111 former Free Churches, only three of which (Duke St., Hope St., and Milton) satisfied the basic requirement. This left areas like Govan and Partick without Free Church provision and the minority argued that, given the enormous transference of Free Church property to the United Free Church, Govan and Partick should be regarded as exceptional cases for which special provision was justified. This view did not prevail with the Commission but the attempt to add weight to it with statistical data gave rise to much contention. The Free Church subsequently erected Gaelic churches in both Partick and Govan by grant-aid from central funds.

In 1908 the Church of Scotland invited the United Free Church to confer with a view to achieving a further union and this union was finally consummated in 1929. Then, as in 1900, a minority declined to enter the Union, electing instead to continue the United Free Church of Scotland. However, none of the Gaelic churches featured in the minority group and so after 1929 Gaelic preaching in Glasgow was to be found only in the Church of Scotland, the Free Church of Scotland and the Free Presbyterian Church founded in 1893. The effect of the Union of 1929 was to accelerate the programme of mergers and linkages between former United Presbyterian congregations, pre-1900 Free Church congregations and Church of Scotland congregations with the result that many of the buildings, the possession of which was so bitterly contested in 1900, became surplus to requirements and were offered for sale on the property market.

5.2   St Columba Gaelic Church of Scotland

Because this congregation belonged to the Established Church
it was unaffected by the Union of 1900. Its history in the first
half of this century has already been published in considerable
detail.[2] The congregation continues to occupy the imposing
building which it erected on St Vincent Street in 1904 and,
despite the fewness of its numbers, a Gaelic service with a
regular attendance of about thirty, is held at 10 a.m. each
Sunday morning — the last church on the Scottish mainland to
have its main service in Gaelic. The accompanying liturgy is
very different from that which characterised the worship of the
Gaelic chapels two centuries ago. Gaelic hymns rather than
Psalms are used for praise. The High Church tradition which
was introduced a century ago is still in evidence and some
church watchers go so far as to say that Druidical as well as
Christian elements feature in the worship. St Columba's may
still claim to be An Comunn Gaidhealach at prayer, but a change
of emphasis followed the induction of the Rev John MacArthur
in 1989.

5.3   Duke Street Free Gaelic Church – subsequently Grant
Street Free Church

In 1900 the Duke Street Free Gaelic congregation declined to
enter the Union and the building on Mains Street was retained
by the Free Church. The minister, the Rev. John Macleod, born
in Skye in 1852 and ordained to Duke Street in 1894, was one
of the 27 ministers who adhered to the Free Church in 1900.
The senior (retired) minister of the congregation, the Rev Evan
Gordon, had allied himself throughout the negotiations with
opposition to the Union but when confronted with the parting
of the ways, he elected to join the United Free Church.

2   J. C. MacGregor, *The History of St Columba Parish Church Glasgow* (Glasgow, 1935).

However, the congregation were unanimously in favour of remaining with the Free Church and the retention of their building was never in dispute. Unfortunately the church was extensively damaged by a fire which occurred on 8 March 1905 but it was rebuilt and continued in use until 1930 when the congregation purchased a church on Grant Street which had become vacant following the merger of Grant Street United Free Church with Shamrock United Free to form Garnethill Church of Scotland. The Grant Street building, formerly St George's Road Free Church, had been erected in 1860 as a Reformed Presbyterian Church.

After 1900 the congregation supported a Gaelic missionary whose field of labour included Bridgeton, Parkhead, Anderston and Broomielaw. In 1906 the Kirk Session agreed that an English service should be held in the hall at 11 a.m. contemporaneously with the Gaelic service being held in the church; but a suggestion to replace, or alternate, Gaelic with English at the time of the evening service was turned down.[3] In 1985 the congregation officially changed its name from Duke Street to Grant Street and in 1987 the main morning service at 11 a.m. was changed to English while Gaelic took the subsidiary place previously given to the English service at 12.15 p.m. The ministers of the congregation in succession to the above mentioned John Macleod (1894-1921) have been the Rev. Andrew Sutherland (1921-1941), the Rev. Alex MacDonald (1942-1962), the Rev. Neil A Macleod (1963-1979) and the Rev. Donald N Macleod, all of them fluent Gaelic speakers with Skye connections. It is probably true to say that among the post-1900 Free Church congregations, Duke Street has been the one most sympathetic to the cultural support of the Gaelic language.

A demolition order was placed on the Grant Street building in 1989 and the congregation worshipped for a time

3 Minutes of Duke Street Free Church Kirk Session, 26 December 1906.

in Renfield St Stephen's Church of Scotland. In 1995 Grant Street united with St Columba Free Church, Govan, under the ministry of the Rev. Donald N. Macleod. The new congregation uses the Govan church building on Briton Street. A Gaelic service is held at 5.00 p.m. on the second Sunday of each month. The average attendance is 30.

5.4   Hope Street Free Gaelic Church – now St Vincent Street Free Church

The Rev. J D MacCulloch who was minister of Hope Street in 1900 was one of the leaders of the anti-union movement. His leadership ensured that his congregation, with few exceptions, followed his example in adhering to the Free Church. However, the building on Waterloo Street which they retained in 1900, they were to lose by fire in 1957. Since then the congregation have followed a nomadic existence. At first they gathered in the nearby Mains Street Church of Scotland (formerly Mains Street Original Secession) located on Blythswood Street. Redevelopment of the Anderston area forced them to vacate that building in 1965 and then followed temporary sojourns in St Matthew's Church, Bath Street, and later in Central Halls, Bath Street. Eventually in 1971 the congregation were able to rent from Glasgow Corporation the 'Greek' Thomson church on St Vincent Street which had been built as a United Presbyterian church in 1859.[4]

Over the years the congregation have experienced more than their share of misfortune and their current situation is scarcely one that befits a congregation owning a prime city-centre site in 1822 or holding capital of £18,000 in 1900. Nevertheless the congregation has continued to enjoy a notable sequence of ministers. A native of Lochcarron, the Rev. John Macleod, O.B.E., (1921-1939) followed the Rev. J D

4   For a brief history of Hope Street Church 1824-1971 see *The Hope Street Story* by Evan G. Macdonald. 22 pp. Published by the congregation 1971.

MacCulloch (1889-1926). Macleod died suddenly in 1939 and in turn was succeeded by another Lochcarron man, the Rev. R A Finlayson (1940-1946). When R A Finlayson was appointed to the Chair of Theology in the Free Church College, he was succeeded by the Rev. Archibald MacDougall (1947-1961) and when ill-health forced MacDougall's resignation in 1961 the congregation decided that circumstances no longer justified the continuance of a Gaelic ministry.

The Rev. A. G. Ross (1962-72) became the first non-Gaelic minister of the congregation. As it happened his successor, the Rev. J. Douglas Macmillan (1974-82) was a charismatic preacher in Gaelic no less than in English and with Argyllshire Gaelic at that for he was a native of Ardnamurchan. But for the former Hope Street congregation, Gaelic was a thing of the past and Douglas Macmillan's Gaelic ministry was exercised outwith his parish bounds. In 1994 the congregation, known since 1971 as St Vincent Street, united with Milton Free Church and continues to worship in St Vincent Street.

5.5   The Highlanders' Memorial United Free Church – subsequently St Matthew's-Highlanders' Memorial and later Netherton St Matthew's Church of Scotland

In view of the fact that the two largest Free Church Gaelic congregations (Duke Street and Hope Street) declined to enter the United Free Church in 1900, it was thought desirable by that church to make provision for Gaelic speakers in Duke Street and Hope Street who were in sympathy with the Union. Consequently the United Free Church set aside for this purpose the former West Free Church to which the Rev Peter Macdonald minister of Stornoway High Church and one-time assistant at Partick Gaelic Free Church was then called as minister. In 1914 the West Church was condemned and the congregation met for two years in Sandyford United Free Church before they were presented with St Peter's purchased as a memorial to the Highlanders who died in the Great War. The congregation then took the name Highlanders' Memorial United Free Church. In 1941 they were united with St Matthew's under the Rev Francis Joseph Maclauchlan, not himself a Gaelic speaker although a grandson of Colin Sinclair one-time minister of Aberdeen Gaelic Chapel. When their church was destroyed by fire in 1952, St Matthew's-Highlanders' Memorial Church of Scotland was united with Netherton as Netherton-St Matthew's. It seems unlikely that a Gaelic ministry in any shape or form survived after 1940.

5.6   Tradeston (Argyle) Gaelic United Free Church

When the Argyle Gaelic Free Church merged with Tradeston Free Church in 1893, the Argyle building on Oswald Street was disposed of. Latterly it belonged to John Lang's Whisky Co. It was demolished in 1927. In 1900 the minister (the Rev Wm Fraser) and congregation of Tradeston/Argyle Free Church elected to join the United Free Church. In 1911 following the death of the Rev John Buchan (father of Lord Tweedsmuir) the congregation of John Knox's U F Church (which had started life as Kirkfield Gorbals Gaelic Church) was merged with Tradeston and the Tradeston church was sold. The Rev. John Ross, a native of Portmahomack and one-time assistant at Ferintosh who had succeeded Wm Fraser at Tradeston in 1906, became minister of the united charge of John Knox and Tradeston and on his translation to Abernethy and Boat of Garton in 1924, John Knox/Tradeston called a Stornoway man, the Rev Malcolm Macleod. On Macleod's translation to Balquhidder he, in turn, was followed by the Rev John Mackay, a native of Carloway, who went from Portree to John Knox's in 1938, becoming minister of Gorbals/John Knox when these congregations were united in 1943. At that time the John Knox building was disposed of in favour of the retention of the Gorbals church. Thus it was that the lineal descendants of Gaelic congregations which both had their roots in Gorbals (Argyle and John Knox/Kirkfield) were again united in Gorbals Parish Church. The ministers, John Ross, Malcolm Macleod and John Mackay, who followed the Rev Wm Fraser, the last minister of Argyle Gaelic, were obviously all Gaelic speakers but whether there was opportunity for them to exercise their language facility in Tradeston/John Knox/Gorbals, seems doubtful. In 1973 the amalgam of four congregations which then constituted Gorbals was linked with the remnants of another six congregations and any vestigial Highland element diluted to vanishing point.

5.7 St Columba United Free Gaelic Govan subsequently St Columba Copland Road Church of Scotland and now New Govan Church of Scotland

At the time of the 1900 church union the minister of St Columba's was the Rev Evan Grant. A Glenurquhart man with previous experience in Argyle Gaelic and Renton Gaelic Mission as well as in Nigg, he elected to enter the Union and his congregation of 450 members and 400 adherents were content to accompany him. Only seven members left in protest and in all not more than 35 persons allied themselves with the Free Church. Few though the opponents of union were, they set about organising Free Church services and even succeeded in obtaining an interim interdict which allowed them possession of St Columba U F Church in May 1905. Consequently the United Free congregation were dispossessed of the church until the Royal Commission in 1907 restored the Winsor Street property to the United Free Church. The congregation remained there until 1930 when, following the Union of 1929, it was merged with Govan Copland Road. The St Columba church was then sold and later demolished. The congregation continued as St Columba-Copland Road under the ministry of the Rev Alex Shaw who had succeeded Evan Grant in 1927.

In 1932 the Gaelic section of the congregation was strengthened by the addition of the Gaelic section of St Kiaran's when that congregation was united with Dean Park to form St Kiaran's-Dean Park. Alex Shaw left for Lairg in 1937 and was succeeded by the noted Gaelic scholar T M Murchison. Under T M Murchison the congregation was united in 1966 with Summertown to form St Columba-Summertown, the Copland Road property being disposed of and demolished. In 1976 it was united with St Kiaran's-Dean Park to form Govan Trinity and it is now part of New Govan. The Gaelic ministry terminated on the retirement of T M Murchison in 1972.

5.8   St Columba Free Gaelic, Govan

The re-emergence of a Free Govan Gaelic congregation began in 1902 when meetings were held in the Trades Hall at 555 Govan Road. The nucleus of the congregation originated from the discontinuance that same year of Gaelic services in the Macdonald Memorial United Free Church. Strength may also have come from the cessation of Hope Street's missionary operations in Plantation. In addition the phenomenon, peculiar to Gaelic congregations, of support from members and adherents of other, even competing, congregations, was much in evidence. It was conceded by the United Free Church that from their own Gaelic Govan congregation there were a considerable number, including six elders, who, "out of convenience, or from their desire for a Gaelic service, or for some other similar reason, made a practice of attending those (Free Church) meetings, especially in the evening, while remaining loyal members of the United Free Church".[5]

5   Report of the Royal Commission on Churches (Scotland), Vol. II Minutes of Evidence and Appendices. Appendix C-50, II, 6. p. 204. (Edinburgh 1905).

In April 1905 the Royal Commission appointed to allocate property between the churches gave the reconstituted Free Gaelic congregation custody of the former St Columba Free Church on Winsor Street. The Free Church congregation then relinquished the Trades Hall and in June 1905 reoccupied their former building whereupon several of the U F elders attached themselves to the Free Church. However, in May 1907 the Commissioners reversed their decision of 1905 and reallocated the church to the United Free congregation. The dispossessed Free congregation then rented the Masonic Hall on Burndyke Street but with the help of financial support from the central funds of the Free Church a new St Columba Free Gaelic Church was erected on Church Street (now Briton Street) in 1910. The first minister of the new church was the Rev Farquhar Matheson who officiated from 1913 until his translation to Stoer in 1920. He was succeeded by the Rev. William Fraser (1924-1938), a Gaelic-speaking Invernesian, and he, in turn, by the Rev. Alexander Macleod (1939-1947), the Rev. Murdo Macaulay (1949-1956), the Rev John Morrison (1958-79) and, most recently, the Rev Colin MacIver (1981), these all being Lewismen. From the commencement of the congregation Gaelic occupied the place of the main morning service (11 a.m.) while English featured at noon and 6 p.m. but about 1982 the Sunday Gaelic service was discontinued. More recently the congregation suffered depletion from the redistribution of the population. The Rev Colin MacIver resigned from the ministry in 1992. In 1995 the congregation united with Grant Street Free Church (see page 68). There is a Gaelic service, attended by an average of 30 people, at 5.00 p.m. on the second Sunday of each month.

5.9   Partick Gaelic United Free Church – now Gardner Street Church of Scotland

In 1900 the minister and congregation of Partick Gaelic Free Church entered the Union. The minister, the Rev Alex Macrae, a notable annalist of the church in the Highlands, was translated to Creich in 1903 as successor to the Rev Dr Aird. He was followed in Partick by the Rev D F Macleod who had previously been in Greenock Gaelic and Avoch. During his ministry a new church built on Gardner Street was opened in 1905. Following the death of Macleod in 1923 the Rev Kenneth Gillies, a native of Applecross, was inducted. His ministry in Gardner Street was to extend over fifty years. Mr Gillies was succeeded by the Rev David MacInnes in 1977, and he, in turn, by the Rev Roderick Morrison, who was called from the High Church, Stornoway, in 1994. Gaelic services with an evangelical emphasis are still maintained in the congregation and about sixty persons attend a weekly Gaelic service held at the close of the Sunday evening English service.

5.10 Partick Highland Free Gaelic Church

In 1900 the Free Church was bereft of church and congregation in Partick. The conservatively inclined members of Partick Gaelic Free Church had earlier taken their departure to the Free Presbyterian Church in 1893 and it was not until 1905 that the continuing Free Church made any attempt to reconstitute itself in Partick. Inaugural Free Church services were held that year and it was subsequently claimed that 100, 200 and 250 persons attended the morning, afternoon and evening services.[6] These figures doubtless represented sympathisers and the curious rather than solid on-the-ground support. In 1907 the Church Commissioners made no allocation of property to the Free Church in Partick although the Free Church

6   *Ibid.*, Minutes of Evidence, p. 126.

had put in a request for Partick-Anderson church. It was not until 1912 that positive steps were taken to establish a Free Gaelic congregation in Partick.

The immediate stimulus to the formation of a Highland Mission which met in the Forresters' Hall at 294 Dumbarton Road, Partick, was a breakaway from Partick Gaelic United Free Church on account of the introduction of an organ.[7] The leader of this group was Donald G Ferguson (subsequently the Rev. D G Ferguson of Kilbrandon Free Church, a native-born St Kildan) and the company, consisting of four elders, three deacons and 21 members, were constituted as a mission under the superintendence of Partick (Crow Road) Free Church Kirk Session. After two years in the Forresters' Hall the mission began to meet at the Sub-way Hall, 166 Dumbarton Road and continued to do so until 1926.

During this time the congregation were served by a succession of missionaries — Roderick J Macleod, Malcolm MacIver and Murdoch Macrae — all of whom subsequently became Free Church ministers in Cross, Lochs and Kinloch respectively. In 1912 the Mission was transferred to the oversight of Hope Street Free Church and on becoming a sanctioned charge in 1924 it called as its first minister the Rev Peter M Chisholm (later of Lochalsh) who had earlier left the Free Presbyterian Church for the Free Church. Throughout his ministry the congregation met in an 'iron' church on Highburgh Road but during the pastorate of the Rev Murdo Campbell (1934-51) the congregation purchased Partick Dowanvale church on Dowanhill Street, made redundant by the union in 1936, of that congregation with Partick High Church of Scotland. Murdo Campbell, on accepting a call to Resolis, was succeeded by the Rev Malcolm Morrison (1954-70) and he, in turn, by the Rev (now Professor) Donald Macleod (1970-78) during whose ministry Gaelic was to be displaced from a central to a peripheral role.

7 Minutes of Partick Highland Free Church Kirk Session, 12 April 1913.

All of these ministers were Lewismen as befitted a congregation which, until recent years, was essentially a Hebridean working class community comprising women in domestic service and men who earned their living from the river, either in the shipyards or as lightermen. Traditionally, Gaelic services were held at 2.30 p.m. (for the convenience of the domestics) and at 6.30 p.m. and this practice continued until 1972 when at the insistence of the then minister—the Rev Donald Macleod — the afternoon Gaelic service was discontinued and the 6.30 p.m. service became an English service with Gaelic following on at 7.45 p.m. This arrangement continued until 1983 when the Gaelic evening service was discontinued. The Gaelic predominance in the worship of the congregation until comparatively recent times is apparent from the fact that an English prayer meeting did not feature in the weekly services until 1975. A weekday evening service in Gaelic continues to be held on a Thursday evening although attendances have now dwindled to a score or so. In the days when whole tenements in Partick were occupied by Gaelic speakers — a feature that persisted until the 1970's — Partick Highland held separate English and Gaelic communion services co-temporaneously in the church and the church hall but when attendances at the Gaelic declined to forty communicants, the Gaelic table was discontinued. Now there is only an English communion service although some preparatory services (as well as the Thanksgiving service on Monday morning) are still conducted in Gaelic. Since 1981 the congregation has been pastored by a Gaelic-speaking Skyeman, the Rev John A Gillies.

5.11 Partick (Crow Road) Free Church.

The pre-1900 Partick Free Church located on Anderson Street was essentially a conservative congregation but under the influence of a young minister it entered the Union in 1900.

However, the House of Lords decision of 1904 gave new heart to some of its more conservatively-minded worshippers and they formed a Free Church congregation hoping thereby to acquire the buildings on Anderson Street. This, in the event, proved to be a vain hope but eventually a new Partick Free Church was erected on Crow Road and opened in 1910. This congregation lacked any Gaelic tradition but, as already noted, there were many Gaelic speakers in Partick and some associated themselves with the Crow Road congregation. It was not until the ministry of the Rev Neil A Macleod (1956-63) that a Gaelic ministry was introduced in the form of a week-night Gaelic service. That tradition was continued by the Rev William Macleod, a Stornoway man inducted to the congregation in 1976. Mr Macleod held a monthly Gaelic service on a Monday evening. This arrangement still prevails under the present minister, the Rev Iain Smith, another Stornoway man who came to the congregation in 1994 after Mr Macleod's translation to Portree. The congregation has never been able to support a Gaelic prayer meeting but, in common with some other non-Gaelic congregations, it holds a Friday night Gaelic service on communion weekends. In former days, if not now, the Crow Road Free Church was sometimes seen as a haven for Free Church worshippers who were uncomfortable with the more exacting requirements of the Glasgow-Lewis congregations. In addition to serving as a safety-net for Partick Highland misfits, it tended to be favoured by some from the professional, as distinct from the working, classes in the Free Church community.

5.12 St Jude's Free Presbyterian Church

The Free Presbyterian Church came into being in 1893 when two Free Church ministers, the Rev Donald Macfarlane of Raasay and the Rev Donald Macdonald of Shieldaig seceded from the Free Church following the passing of the 1892 Declaratory Act, the intended effect of which was to relax the Free Church's adherence to the Westminster Confession of Faith and so prepare the way for union with the United Presbyterian Church. Several divinity students attached themselves to the new body, among them Neil Cameron, an Argyllshire man who in 1893 was an assistant to the Rev Evan Gordon, minister of Duke Street Free Church. On the formation of the Free Presbyterian Church many of the most conservative worshippers in Duke Street and Partick Gaelic Free Churches, seceded and formed a congregation to which, in 1896, Neil Cameron was called as minister. This congregation of several hundred persons bought a redundant English Episcopal church situated at the corner of Pitt Street and West George Street and, retaining the name of that church, became known as St Jude's Free Presbyterian Church. In the mid-seventies the congregation bought the redundant Woodlands Church of Scotland to which they then transferred carrying the name St Jude's.

Neil Cameron, as minister of St Jude's, preached in English and Gaelic until his death in 1932 when he was succeeded by the Rev Roderick Mackenzie who likewise preached in English and Gaelic until 1945 when he was made *persona non grata* by the Free Presbyterian Synod for affirming that a minister had a right of protest against the Synod's decisions. On resigning his charge Mackenzie was followed by the Rev D J Matheson, a member of a noted ministerial family that in 1975 furnished a Moderator (Dr James G Matheson) for the Church of Scotland General Assembly. He in turn was succeeded by the Rev Donald Maclean and Gaelic preaching has been maintained down the years in St Jude's.

5.13   Free Presbyterian Relief Congregation

The Free Presbyterian Relief Congregation came into existence in 1945 as a result of disputes within the Free Presbyterian Church during the period 1938-1945. These disputes
centred on the question of whether a protest against a decision
of the Church's Supreme Court (the Synod) *ipso facto* sepa-
rated the protester from the Church. The Rev R Mackenzie,
minister of St Jude's Free Presbyterian Church, Glasgow, held
that it did not. In this he was supported by elders and members
both from his own congregation and from elsewhere. In May
1945 the Free Presbyterian Synod required that Mr Mackenzie
withdraw from his position by the end of November 1945,
failing which he would not be considered after that date to be a
minister of the Free Presbyterian Church. Mr Mackenzie did
not withdraw and those who continued to support him organ-
ised services which were held at first (1945-46) in the Y.M.C.A.,
Bothwell Street and later (1946-55) in the Original Secession
Church, Broomielaw. During this period in rented premises
there were no regular Gaelic services but with the purchase of
property at 202 Renfrew Street in 1955 Mr Mackenzie, who
had been preaching regularly in English but without any
administration of the Sacraments, began holding Gaelic
services in addition. An afternoon Gaelic service was held each
Sunday at 2 pm and a Gaelic prayer meeting was held on
Tuesdays at 7.30 pm. With the death of Mr Mackenzie in
August 1972 the prayer meeting lapsed but the Sunday service
continued to be held until 1982. The congregation was
disbanded in January 1985.

6   THE EBB-TIDE

6.1   Anglicized and lapsed Highlanders

It was early in the 19th century that the tide began to ebb in Glasgow's Gaelic churches. Four Gaelic congregations would appear to represent the high water mark of popular demand for Gaelic services even at a time (1855) when as many as 50,000 Highlanders were said to be resident in the city. In 1823 Kirkfield (Gorbals) Gaelic chapel correctly predicted its own demise as a Gaelic church in the event of Hope Street chapel becoming established. The post-1850 proliferation of Gaelic services was not so much a response to popular demand as an oversupply actuated by missionary and denominational considerations. The churches, particularly the Free Church Highland Committee, strove to repeat within the urban Highland community the church growth that was then keeping pace with Glasgow's Westward-migrating population; but their efforts proved unavailing.

One of the major difficulties confronting the Gaelic congregations was the problem of retaining the loyalty of the rising generation — a problem that dogged the Gaelic church in all of Scotland's cities. Children born in the city grew up in ignorance of the Gaelic language and to provide for the needs of these children and so retain the whole family within the one congregation, the Gaelic congregations had to introduce English services at a very early stage. This was entirely in keeping with the church's primary commitment which was to promote the interests of religion rather than Gaelic but it was resisted by the Celtic purists who thought that "the preaching is not worth a hearing if it is not in Gaelic". No satisfactory *modus vivendi* was ever attained. Perhaps none was possible but the consequence was that it proved to be exceedingly difficult to build up and retain family loyalty. The tendency was for the second generation, if it retained a church connection at all, to become attached to one of the English congregations proliferating in Glasgow's suburbs. Not infrequently young married men in membership of a Gaelic congregation requested disjunction certificates for the reason that their wives did not understand Gaelic and so could not worship with them in the Gaelic church.The vitality of the Gaelic congregation was sapped by this unending exodus and the congregation became dependent on a continued influx of newcomers, mostly domestic servants and labourers, to sustain its life.

The new arrivals were usually to be found in the poorest part of the city centre, in ghettos associated with industry as in Springburn and Gorbals, or with shipping as in Govan or Broomielaw. There was thus no incentive for the Gaelic congregation to emulate the English congregation and migrate Westward with the more affluent members of society. Indeed, the pressure was to stay where they were and hope that some of those who had moved to the suburbs would retain their connection with city-centre churches. Perhaps the introduction in 1872 of Sunday transport encouraged this development. At any rate when the city-centre Gaelic churches found it expedient (as all of them did) to vacate their old building, they selected another site or empty church as near as possible to their former location. Following the population dispersal that occurred in the mid-twentieth century, these churches became heavily dependent on Sunday transport to maintain their numbers and the later discontinuance of the Subway on Sundays had a serious effect on attendances as, for instance, at Govan Free Gaelic Church.

Intermarriage, mono-lingual wives and children and the shifting population were not the only adverse factors that weakened the Gaelic congregations. There was also a rapidly increasing secularism and indifference to spiritual values in the urban society. In response to this growing worldliness the church sought to utilise Gaelic to its own advantage. By 1850 it no longer needed to have recourse to Gaelic to make its message intelligible either to the faithful or to the careless but it viewed Gaelic preaching and Gaelic fellowship as offering a more hopeful avenue of evangelism to those who could be reached that way. The emphasis therefore shifted from Gaelic as the *sine qua non* for worship to Gaelic as the means of evangelism. The territorial principle was put into effect and missionaries deployed in strategic areas. But, although official circles were reluctant to say so, the results of this outreach were mostly meagre and disappointing. The missionary had, of course, to justify his stewardship and while some reports were said to "afford ample grounds for encouragement" or "were such as to encourage in perseverance and further diligence", it was conceded that "the cases of undoubted blessing are still few".[1] The fact was that, notwithstanding the enthusiasm with which the Highland church pursued the lapsed, the Highlander in the city was becoming more and more indifferent to the exhortations and consolations of the Gospel, in Gaelic no less than in English. The simplicity of life and seriousness of outlook which, to an extent, characterised the Highlander in his native glen, had been displaced by the complexity of life and vanity of purpose associated with urban living. The restraining and conformist influences of a tightly-knit island or glen community were removed by the anonymity of city life and a sizeable proportion of the city-dwelling Highlanders became detached from, and unreachable by, the Church. Gaelic outreach proved to be no more effective than English. The world and its ways had become too attractive.

---

1   SRO, CH. 16/3/2/3, Hope Street Free Gaelic Kirk Session Minutes, 12 April and 4 July 1893.

6.2 The Spirit of a New Age

Contemporaneously with this growing public indifference and detachment, a more liberal outlook was penetrating the church itself. An ebb-tide of another kind had set in. Duncan Campbell, the minister of Moulin (Pitlochry), describing in the New Statistical Account the moral and religious outlook of his parishioners wrote in 1845, "Spurious liberalism and soul-withering infidelity have as yet made little progress among us. But it is much to be dreaded that the never ceasing intercourse with this district and the large manufacturing towns in the South may eventually lead to the introduction and diffusion of sentiments and opinions which tend to poison the mind and unhinge the better principles of the people".[2] The Gaelic church, living in the city centre and surrounded by a greater laxity of opinion and liberty of conduct, was not immune to change. The spirit of the new age had already made itself felt in the wider church, both theologically and liturgically, and the urban Gaelic church was not unaffected by the spirit that was abroad. Ripples of theological controversies that had agitated the higher courts of the church could be discerned in the comparative backwater of Hope Street Gaelic church. In 1845 a deacon resigned his office on the grounds that "he now believed in universal atonement and other kindred doctrines".[3] In 1863 exception was taken to the ordination of a prospective deacon because it was alleged that he held defective views on the inspiration of scripture. Apparently, in arguing in favour of the use of hymns along with the Psalms, he had been so carried away with enthusiasm for the hymn-writers' achievements that he had rashly affirmed "all poets are equally inspired".[4] The Kirk Session after a lengthy debate, reached a non-proven verdict and the man was ordained.

2   The *New Statistical Account of Scotland* (Edinburgh, 1845) Vol. X p. 653.
3   SRO, CH. 16/3/2/1, Minutes of Hope Street Free Gaelic Kirk Session,25 June 1845, p. 24.
4   *Ibid.*, 9 January 1863, p. 16.

Advocacy of the use of hymns in worship, the formation of choirs and the introduction of congregational soirees were generally regarded by conservative office-bearers as indicators of liberalising tendencies. Evidently the use of hymns was under consideration in Hope Street as early as 1863. It is not clear when they were introduced but in 1872 the Hope Street Kirk Session specified the duties of the precentor as "adopting tunes suited to the peculiar nature of the Psalms and hymns which the minister may select".[5] In 1884 Argyle Gaelic church agreed to "the judicious use of hymns" at the Bible Class.[6] Some viewed the introduction of hymns with their heterogeneous theology as potentially a greater threat to the church's orthodoxy than the introduction of instrumental music. Paradoxically, however, both Hope Street and Argyle petitioned the Free Church General Assembly against allowing the use of instrumental music in 1883 (the year that the Assembly first sanctioned the practice) and the Assembly's approval led to the resignation of some Hope Street elders. Argyle Gaelic church agreed in 1873 to reserving space for a choir. Hope Street already had a choir but, on objections being raised, it was disbanded in 1875.[7] However, a groundswell in its favour persisted and in 1889 the Hope Street precentor dissociated himself from a *de facto* attempt by would-be choristers to reconstitute the choir by sitting together near the precentor's desk.[8] Clearly hymns, choirs and organs were all points of tension in the Gaelic churches with the conservatives viewing the proposed changes as indicative of a decadent tendency. Similarly soirees were seen by some as a digression from the

---

5   *Ibid.*, 22 September 1872.

6   SRO, CH. 3/1298/3, Minutes of Argyle Free Gaelic Church Kirk Session, 23 December 1884.

7   SRO, CH. 16/3/2/2, Minutes of Hope Street Free Gaelic Kirk Session, 23 June 1875.

8   *Ibid.*, 29 April 1889. Choristers taking the law into their own hands in this way in order to force a recalcitrant Kirk Session was, apparently, a common practice, see A. F. Forrest, *Our Fifty Years*. The Jubilee Book of Renfield Street United Presbyterian Church, Glasgow (Glasgow, 1898), p. 16.

church's true function. Govan Gaelic instituted soirees in 1867 and by 1886 they were being run as full-blown concerts with tickets for admission. Hope Street agreed, in response to popular demand, to soirees in 1861 but possibly a reaction set in for, thirty years later, at the induction of J D MacCulloch, some office-bearers expressed their opposition to arrangements for "a social meeting at which a plain cup of tea would be served to such as chose to have one".[9] Such opposition was typical of the attitude of those who felt that creature comforts of any kind were incompatible with the serious business of worship. For instance in 1862 Hope Street office-bearers were embroiled in a controversy over the installation of heating apparatus in the church. While this proposal was hotly opposed, ostensibly on the grounds of expense, in the view of the Presbytery the underlying reason had more to do with maintaining an unreasonably Spartan attitude to worship.

6.3 The Gaelic Church and Celtic Culture

As the exclusive emphasis on preaching and religious instruction was relaxed, so more emphasis came to be placed on the role of the church in promoting Gaelic culture. In the 1860's a Celtic debating society was meeting in Hope Street Free Gaelic church and in 1876 the church instituted evening classes in Gaelic. St Columba's Gaelic church had its dramatic society and Celtic music featured prominently in congregational activities. When the congregation formed a Gaelic choir in 1875 it was found that "Psalm tunes were not sufficient to sustain interest and Gaelic songs in four part harmony were introduced and practised assiduously".[10] Eventually, "the Choir became famous as the foremost organisation of its kind in Gaelic secular music".[11] By such happenings, in the most visible

---

9   SRO, CH. 16/3/3/3, Minutes of Hope Street Free Gaelic Deacons' Court, 8 April 1889.
10   J. C. MacGregor, *The History of St Columba Parish Church Glasgow* (Glasgow,1935), p 49.
11   *Ibid.*, p. 71.

visible sector of the urban Gaelic church, the Gaelic language became not so much an adjunct to the church's mission as a beneficiary of the church's patronage. The Gaelic church had assumed the role of patron of Celtic culture.

This interest in the cultural heritage was certainly a reversal of the church's traditional attitude to Celtic music and song. Many twentieth century writers have asserted that religion in Scotland has been a life-destroying rather than a life-affirming influence. In the Highlands especially, Presbyterianism has been castigated for its alleged influence on its followers, "clouding the spirit, stultifying the mind, taking away all joyousness and light-hearted gaiety, laying a ban upon music, even upon songs, making laughter as rare as a clansman landlord".[12] Such a view represents a caricature of the church's influence on the Highland people but like every exaggeration it contains an element of truth. In the early nineteenth century when the evangelical church emerged from the twilight of Celtic mysticism and Highland Moderatism, it unhesitatingly repudiated the people's cultural heritage. Continued association with Highland folk-literature and the traditional means of communicating it, was proscribed as being conducive to the survival of superstition. The church seemed determined to effect a total separation between the sacred and the secular. (Incidentally, the conviction that merriment in general came from the devil himself, was not confined to the Highland church; it was held by Presbyterians of all kinds both North and South of the Highland line).[13] In retrospect the exclusiveness insisted on by the Highland clergy was almost certainly a serious misjudgment for, as MacInnes has pointed out, man cannot live without a secular culture and it would have been wiser for the church to have endeavoured to purify the culture instead of withdrawing

---

12 Wm Sharp (Fiona Macleod), The Gael and His Heritage, THE NINETEENTH CENTURY, November 1900, reprinted in *The Winged Destiny* (London, 1927), p. 235.

13 Wm Robertson Nicoll, *The Day Book of Claudius Clear* (London, 1905) p. 347.

from it.[14] Perhaps the church was afraid that the folk-culture—its music and literature — had such an irresistible appeal to the Highland heart that nothing short of a total rejection of it was compatible with the new evangelicalism. This indeed was the attitude of such influential leaders of the Highland church as Dr John MacDonald of Ferintosh and Dr Alex Stewart of Dingwall both of whom were themselves deeply attached to, and strongly attracted by, the folk-culture. But whatever the reason, the religious Highlander disowned his cultural heritage not only in respect of the worship of the church but also with regard to the everyday life of the Christian community. The consequences are with us to this day. As Donald Macleod has pointed out, there remains a great divide between cultural pursuits and evangelical Hebridean Christianity with nothing between the bothan and the prayer meeting to enlist the allegiance of ardent hearts.[15]

Religion was not the only influence that lay behind the rejection of the Gaelic culture last century. Equally determinative was the desire on the part of many young, image-conscious Gaelic speakers to be wholly assimilated into an English-speaking lifestyle. They considered it to be more trendy to ignore their Gaelic background and those in this category who were content to retain a church connection found that membership of a non-Gaelic congregation better suited their outlook. On the other hand, there were also those whose primary concern it was to reject the church rather than the culture. This was the view largely adopted by the mid-twentieth century elitist Gaelic community. Whatever recognition the church might have received on ceremonial occasions, its mission was generally scorned by the Gaelic literati but this may now be changing. The Gaelic church has seldom experi-

14 J. MacInnes, *The Evangelical Movement in the Highlands of Scotland, 1688-1800* (Aberdeen, 1951), p. 60.
15 *Stornoway Gazette.* April 8, 1989

enced an easy relationship with society's opinion-formers. At one time or another it has come under attack for its attitude either to the language or to the culture. Whatever the church's misjudgments may have been with regard to the acceptability of folk-culture in a Christian community, at no time did the leaders of the Gaelic church show any antipathy to the language itself. As long as there was any possibility of reaching the people more effectively through the medium of Gaelic, the Highland church was anxious to use it. More than that, the church acknowledged its indebtedness to the language. When others urged its eradication as a hindrance to the progress of civilisation, the minister of Inverness Free East Church countered that it would ill become the Free Church to lay a hand on it if only because the language had shielded the Highlanders from heretical and dissenting opinions. The Gaelic language, he claimed, had been a "line of circumvallation that had prevented many sectaries from entering the Highlands". [16]

16   Proceedings of the Free Church of Scotland General Assembly 22 May 1858, p. 60.

7   THE THINGS THAT REMAIN AND ARE READY TO DIE

7.1   Worship Past and Present

An eighteenth century worshipper entering one of the conservative Highland congregations still to be found in Scotland's cities would not feel unfamiliar with the proceedings, for the form of worship practised there has scarcely changed with the passing of the centuries. In this respect Highland (mainly Free Church) congregations have acquired a distinction which was not always theirs. When the first Gaelic chapel opened in Glasgow in 1770 the only difference between the worship in the Gaelic church and that of its English (or Lowland) counterpart was the language itself. At that time worship in the Established Church followed a uniform style as laid down in the Westminster Directory of Public Worship and the liturgy or mode of worship of the Gaelic chapels did not differ in any significant respect from that to be found in the parish churches throughout the land. The church, both Gaelic and English, was one in doctrine, government and worship. Only the language distinguished the Gaelic chapel. Before long, of course, the Gaelic churches had to introduce English services but as the language disparity began to disappear other differences, both theological and liturgical, became established. The trend towards a less rigid adherence to the theology and form of worship set forth in the Westminster Standards gradually enveloped virtually all of the Lowland congregations including even some which were of Highland or Hebridean origin or complexion. At the present time only those congregations belonging to the minority conservative denominations — the Free Church of Scotland, the Reformed Presbyterian and the Free Presbyterian Churches — are required to retain the form of worship and confessional subscription adopted by the Church of Scotland at the Reformation.

The liturgy of the Reformed Church, in contradistinction to that of the Roman Church, emphasised what could be heard rather than what could be seen. Scripture exposition held the centre stage and still does although nowadays the sermon seldom exceeds one hour, its being generally conceded that if the hearer did not benefit from the first hour he was unlikely to do so thereafter. The importance of the Bible as the focal point of worship was traditionally symbolised by the carrying in of the pulpit Bible before the minister entered the pulpit. This practice is still maintained in some churches and the injunction 'Let us hear the Word of God' which prefaces the Scripture reading is held by some as being the most solemn point of the service.

To the uninitiated the most distinctive feature of the worship of Glasgow's vestigial Gaelic churches is the absence of instrumental music and the fact that the congregation stands for prayer while remaining seated for praise. The prayer is always delivered extemporary and may occupy ten minutes, sometimes longer. Although it is not read, it is to a large extent composed of familiar phrases and makes generous use of biblical verses. If its tone is not very different from that of earlier days its length most certainly is. It was said of the Rev James McLauchlan, one-time minister of Edinburgh Gaelic Chapel and later of Moy, that it was his regular practice to give one hour to the opening prayer.[1] A prayer of such immoderate length could not of course be confined simply to confession of sin, general thanksgiving for mercies enjoyed and supplication for grace with which to meet the trials and sorrows of the coming week. Instead it ranged over the whole body of revealed truth from before the foundation of the world to the day of judgment. From the lips of a gifted practitioner this was not always a gross imposition on the hearers. John Campbell an ironmonger renowned for his evangelistic tours of the Highlands said of a

1   W. K. Leask, *Dr Thomas M'Lauchlan* (Edinburgh, 1905), p. 138.

fellowship meeting which he attended in Inverness in 1797 that it "began at nine at night and William Fraser prayed more than an hour. But such a prayer! Another hour of it would have been no burden to either a Christian or a poet". [2] Sometimes, however, it was difficult to distinguish prayer from preaching. Blurring of the lines of demarcation was not uncommon. In 1843, one spirited detractor of the Disruption Church accused the Rev. Alex Flyter of Alness (one of the Ross-shire luminaries of the Free Church) of making a translation of the sermon he delivered at the Gaelic service serve as the opening prayer of the succeeding English service. [3] The advice offered by the critic as a corrective to the tendency to confuse preaching with prayer was for the Free Church to adopt the Anglican Book of Common Prayer. In the present century the trend to shorter prayers has helped to eliminate extraneous elements.

Praise in Free Church congregations still excludes what are officially termed 'non-canonical materials of praise'. In practice singing is restricted to the Psalms of David in metre. One change that has become established since the nineteenth century is the   discontinuance of 'lining out', the practice whereby the precentor intones each line of the Psalm on a recitative note before the congregation joins in with the melody. This was the common practice both in English and in Gaelic two centuries ago but with increasing literacy the need for it ended (if, indeed, it ever existed) and the practice was discarded in English Psalmody although retained in Gaelic. The cessation of lining out did not lead, as might have been expected, to an increase in the number of verses sung and the custom remains for only a selected few verses to be sung. The complete Psalter as a manual of praise is honoured more in the breach than in the observance. Contrary to the practice of the Anglican Church, the range of verses selected for congrega-

2   R Philip, *The Life, Times and Missionary Enterprises of the Rev. John Campbell* (London,1841), p. 336.

3   R Walker, *Expostulatory Letters to Free Church Ministers* (Edinburgh, 1846), pp. 85-86.

tional praise tends to be very restricted. It used to be custom-
ary for the minister to read through the verses to be sung but
many now only read the first verse or less. The biographer of
Duncan Campbell of Kiltearn (1796-1873), describing the
Psalms which Campbell favoured for congregational praise,
refers to "his grave measured insistence in reading them", the
tone and look of appropriation with which he read making
evident the meaningfulness of the verses to himself.[4] James
Beattie, writing in 1778, took the view that for a minister to
omit expressive reading of the verses to be sung could not fail
"to lessen the veneration of the people for that part of
worship".[5] Whether or not he was correct in his surmise, it is
true that in many city congregations there is a pronounced
lack of fervour in the praise. Although the choice of tunes is
the prerogative of the preacher most ministers allow the
precentor freedom to select the tunes and the latter is well-
advised to confine his choice to those appreciated by the
congregation. For the most part the sacred melodies, like the
verses, have not changed down the centuries and the sound of
hallowed cadences that rise and fall under the sensitive direction of a skilled precentor can be as uplifting to the spirits of
present-day worshippers as it was to those who sang the self-
same songs in days gone by.

Just such a spirit of restrained exhilaration is evident at
the twice yearly celebration of the Lord's Supper. Here again
the time-honoured practices are, for the most part, still
maintained. Preparatory services for the purpose of self-
examination and humiliation are held from Thursday to Saturday preceding the Communion Sunday and a Monday thanksgiving service, at which the mood is usually less oppressive,
concludes the Communion season. A question-meeting at which
the leading male communicants are invited to illustrate the

4   Duncan MacGregor, *Campbell of Kiltearn* (Edinburgh, 1874), pp. 37-39.
5   Quoted by C.G. M'Crie, *The Public Worship of Presbyterian Scotland* (Edinburgh, 1892),
     p. 314.

relevance of a given verse of Scripture in the context of their own spiritual pilgrimage still features in the services of some congregations. Admission to the Lord's Table is open to all who are members in good standing in any congregation and communion tokens are handed out and taken up by way of regulating admission to the table. Fencing of the table continues to have its place, the purpose of that practice being not just to discourage and exclude those whose conduct may be inconsistent with a Christian profession but also to encourage and include those whose doubts and fears needlessly inhibit them from coming forward. While verses from Psalm 118 are being sung to the tune Coleshill, a solemn air for ever associated in the minds of the worshippers with the dying of the Lord Jesus, the symbols of his broken body and shed blood are carried by the elders to the serving table, the common cup, usually of goblet design, containing fermented wine and the silver plate subtending slices of bread enfolded in a linen napkin. Two ministers officiate at the administration of the sacrament, first serving the elders who in turn serve the people. Table addresses in the form of a word of reassurance prior to the distribution of the elements and a word of exhortation following participation, round off the preaching. Having thus renewed their vows, the communicants rise from the table solemnised by the remembrance of Christ's finished work of atonement. A sense of reverence and seriousness of purpose characterises the sacramental worship in these one-time Gaelic churches.

The mood of sober earnestness is equally noticeable at the midweek meeting for corporate prayer. This meeting when conducted in accordance with the traditional rites of Highland Christianity has a certain distinctiveness which may well be unique in Christendom. Whereas in most prayer groups the decision whether or not to engage in prayer is left to the whim of the individual with virtually no one being excluded on the grounds of gender or giftedness, the Highland church prayer meeting is conducted on quite different lines. Instead of allowing open prayer, the minister or presiding layman invites selected individuals to lead in prayer. No one is expected to articulate even a brief prayer without being called on by name and those who are 'put up' are not expected to demur. The invitation to lead in prayer is addressed to men only, precedence sometimes, but not always, being accorded to the office-bearers. In theory all male communicant members are regarded as eligible to lead in prayer, but the choice is left to the presiding authority. It is very difficult to discover any documentary or historical material having a bearing on when or why this type of prayer meeting developed. Certainly it provides in theory at least, for the exclusion of those whose contribution tends to self-assertion or is otherwise unsuitable. On the other hand, it has little regard to the frame of mind of the individual who is expected to impart spiritual leadership regardless of whether he feels up to it or not.

7.2   Pulpit and Pew

A feature of church attendance in times past—one liable to be overlooked nowadays—is that it was a mixed multitude which comprised most Highland congregations. The congregation certainly was not a homogeneous gathering of the faithful, any homogeneity tended to be of a communal rather than a spiritual character. The saved and the unsaved could well have been represented in roughly equal numbers. The committed and the devout were obviously present as were the unsure and the anxious. But many of the worshippers would have been indifferent to spiritual realities and some among them actually sceptical, or even hostile to the message proclaimed from the pulpit. The reasons that prompted unbelievers to attend church were multifarious. They ranged from the need for companionship and the desire for entertainment to the lurking suspicion that it was good for the soul to be exposed to the wholesome admonitions handed out so unsparingly by the pulpiteers. Whatever the reason, the evening diet of worship was generally favoured by the non-religious worshipper. Last century the street corner was virtually the only alternative to the church as a Sunday meeting place for social intercourse and a congregation which tended to be identified with a given Highland community (such as Skye or Lewis) was the obvious place in which to meet relatives or acquaintances. In this regard the Gaelic churches fulfilled a useful social role in the life of the community. Similarly in an age when live entertainment was confined to the local playhouse the pulpit had considerable drawing power for Highlanders who had been reared in an atmosphere of clerical rhetoric.

The Presbyterian church in its reformed purity repudiated the use of the arts—visual or instrumental—in worship because of the tendency of such artistic activity to bemuse the mind. But an exception was allowed in respect of the art of rhetoric and many preachers such as Macdonald of Ferintosh or Kennedy of Dingwall could achieve a standard of dramatic performance that was little short of spellbinding. To be carried along under the sway of hypnotic preaching and brought inexorably and irresistibly to the edge of everlasting perdition only to escape to a High Street peopled with familiar faces was to undergo a catharsis that was soothing to the soul; and many there were who welcomed the opportunity to peer into an abyss from which deliverance was still possible. But not all preaching fell into that category.

Most sermons had a doctrinal rather than a dramatic content and were intended to instruct more than to alarm. The instruction was with respect to the way of salvation (*ordo salutis*) and was primarily directed at the unconverted. Exhorting professed believers with regard to practical godliness and the exercise of piety in the minutiae of daily life did not feature prominently in pulpit work. This may have been due in part to a restricted range of 'ethical' vocabulary in the Gaelic language but the judgment is probably equally true of English sermons by Gaelic ministers; and so the avoidance of specific applications to the ordinary concerns of daily living may be seen as a characteristic of the Highland pulpit. However, it would be wrong to suppose that the Christian conduct of church members was not a matter of real concern to ecclesiastical authority. On the contrary, "a verbal profession of faith was held of little account if it did not coexist with a life that could bear the scrutiny of friend and foe".[6] The overall emphasis was strongly evangelical with the accent falling on edification rather than entertainment, and exegesis rather than ritual. This intellectual emphasis did not, of course, preclude a conjunct appeal to the heart and there were few notable Highland preachers who did not possess the ability to move men's hearts by the tenderness, earnestness and winsomeness of their preaching. The widespread notion that the typical Highland minister was some "grim philosopher affirming the vanity of life" is a gross distortion of the Gaelic pulpit for the ministerial gift most widely esteemed by the people was what was known as 'unction', a property which characterised the preaching of a few ministers most of the time and others on more rare occasions. The exercise of this gift lifted the congregation to a peak of spiritual fervour giving the people a new awareness of things unseen and eternal and causing them "to think of other things".[7] With hearts and minds solemnised by such awe-inspiring preaching the worshippers took their homeward journey well satisfied with the preacher's endeavours.

The 'sermon-tasting' mentality was very much in evidence in the nineteenth century and possibly even more so in the twentieth century. In addition to the office-bearers who

6   John Mackay, *The Church in the Highlands* (London, 1914), p. 266.
7   A. C. Cheyne, *The Transforming of the Kirk* (Edinburgh, 1983) p. 34.

obviously were inhibited from what the old seceders termed "promiscuous hearing" every congregation had its loyal core of membership who could be relied on to be in their seats week by week; but there was also a large body of floating hearers whose attendance at one church or another was determined by the preacher for the day. This practice was less in evidence in the early days of the Gaelic chapels when most pews were rented and pew-renters were generally to be found in their allotted space. With the passing of the years the number of churches increased, pew occupancy fell and the quality of preaching became more variable. All of these factors encouraged a nomadic tendency to develop especially among uncommitted hearers. In the twentieth century peripatetic wandering was further encouraged by the availability of transport—both public and private. Consequently the pull of a powerful preacher in one or two congregations had an adverse affect on attendances elsewhere. Furthermore the practice of inviting visiting preachers to communion services also ensured that the ranks of the faithful would be swollen with roving worshippers in proportion to the popularity of the preacher. And the custom whereby, in this century, Free Church Gaelic congregations celebrated communion in rotation instead of contemporaneously further reinforced itinerant worship.

Both in the pulpit and the pew the Highland church was rich in men of memorable, not to say eccentric, character and the exploits of many of these worthies have become enshrined in the folklore of Highland religion. Any preacher such as David Carment of Duke Street who had the reputation of being a good entertainer was assured of a crowded, if not always discerning, congregation. The religious Highlander was strongly attracted to ministerial personalities perhaps especially to such as gave evidence of being 'far ben' or possessing 'nearness to God'. Men such as Macdonald of Ferintosh, Kennedy of Dingwall, Sage of Resolis, Fraser of Kirkhill and

Mackintosh of Tain, were immensely popular. Kennedy was nominated for every vacant Gaelic charge both in Glasgow and the other Lowland cities. The attraction of their preaching lay in its biblical-centredness, the function of the minister being primarily that of ministering to the spiritual necessities of life, dispensing the Water of Life to the spiritually thirsty and the Bread of Life to the spiritually hungry. There was also a prominent emphasis given to what was termed experimental preaching — experimental not in the modern sense of innovative but in the sense of having to do with the experience — the frames and feelings — of the worshipper. Experimental preaching was both subjective and objective; objective in its emphasis on biblical truth such as the doctrine of the atonement but subjective in its application of that truth to the experience of the individual. Although far from being the intention of the preacher, this sometimes gave rise, in the mind of the hearer, to undue self-examination with the subjective feelings of the individual assuming a more decisive role than the objective truth of the atonement. This in turn led to a lack of assurance concerning personal salvation and a reluctance to make any profession of faith, its being considered overly presumptuous so to do. The result was that many people of transparent piety never became communicant members of the Gaelic congregations.

A feature that was peculiar to Highland Christianity particularly in the Northern Highlands was the reputed ability of the pious to discern from a verse of Scripture brought before their mind in prayer, the will of God with regard to the outcome of a particular issue that had exercised their hearts whether that issue had to do with some proposed action concerning themselves or even the eternal destiny of some individual whose case had come to their notice. Dr Kennedy of Dingwall was a staunch believer in the reality of this divine intimation which he termed 'the secret of the Lord'. As he put it, "To the case thus presented, the Lord may apply a passage of Scripture to indicate his mind regarding it, and to give to the pleader a favourable or unfavourable anticipation of the result".[8] Kennedy disallowed any prophetic claim for this supernatural gift but viewed it as an assured premonition resulting from "an adaptation by God himself of his own written word". The pious (some would say credulous) people in the Highlands came to view authentic occurrences of this nature as endowing with divine accreditation the messenger's ministry and men who failed to manifest the gift were regarded as operating on a lower level of spiritual achievement. In its most exaggerated form these supernatural intimations were almost commonplace among the 'men' of Caithness but there is no record of the gift being in evidence in Glasgow's Highland congregations.

From the mid-nineteenth century when congregations were given the power to appoint their own office-bearers, the men ordained to office in the Gaelic churches were, as far as can be ascertained, representative of the social groups comprising the congregation. Clearly the more educated a man was, the more he could contribute to the administrative work of the congregation and, other things being equal, men with literate or numerate qualities were regarded as especially useful. But the prime qualification was a man's spiritual qualities and the fact that he may have been illiterate did not disqualify him from office. In some Lowland Gaelic congregations office-bearers were to be found who could not sign their name. Since many of the Gaelic congregations were mainly working-class congregations it was inevitable that office-bearers had to be recruited from the lower socio-economic classes.

The main concern then, as now, was not that the elders would "look good on paper" but that they would be able to deputise for the minister in respect of pastoral care. The minimal requirement would be the ability to pray with the sick and

8 John Kennedy, *The Days of the Fathers in Ross-shire* (Inverness, 1927) new and enlarged edition, p. 253.

the housebound and to conduct family worship in the homes of the people if requested. Then, as now, it would be taken for granted that office-bearers in a Gaelic congregation would be in the habit of conducting family worship in their own homes after the manner so memorably portrayed by Robert Burns in *The Cottar's Saturday Night*. They would also be expected to lead in prayer at the congregational prayer meeting. This could be a major test of a man's spiritual vitality for if he was neglectful of his own spiritual wellbeing it was difficult to conceal the fact for long. A lack of facility in prayer reflected lack of practice. The problem of course could be compounded by expecting men to pray in English who habitually prayed in Gaelic and a major reason for the failure of some congregations timeously to replace Gaelic services with English was the reluctance on the part of the office-bearers to take part in an English prayer meeting. Even in recent years Glasgow still had its complement of Gaelic elders who could pray in Gaelic but not in English.

7.3 Home and Family

One form of indoctrination once widely employed throughout the church but which has now passed into desuetude is the practice of catechising. This was a learning system involving question and answer based primarily, but not exclusively, on a doctrinal manual. It was systematic with respect both to the doctrine presented and the persons instructed. In post-reformation times the people were gathered in the church either on Sunday or on weekdays but in Highland parishes in later times the scattered population made it necessary for the minister to catechise the people in their separate localities. On his arrival all the families in the district would gather together in one home or barn whereupon the minister would proceed to "reprove, rebuke and exhort with all long-suffering and doctrine". Donald Sage with characteristic assurance, confidently affirmed in his *Memorabilia Domestica* that he found such a visitation "to be at once satisfactory to myself and edifying and acceptable to the people". Contrary to what is sometimes imagined the practice was generally popular with the people and it gave the ministers the opportunity to speak to them in a more direct and personal manner than was either possible or expedient from the pulpit. The dialogue that developed between minister and people was full of interest and instruction for all parties including the minister. A minister skilled in the art of catechising could take even a silly answer and turn it to advantage without embarrassment to anyone. One such was Robert Finlayson, latterly of Helmsdale, who could "use the answer, whatever its character, as the text of a fresh and helpful homily. Thus the stupidest answerer felt he contributed to the spiritual cheer".[9] And spiritual cheer was what catechising was designed to achieve. To the extent that pastoral visitation of people in their homes is still maintained it now takes more the form of an exchange of pleasantries than an exhortation to godliness but in many homes a Scripture reading and prayer is still considered *de rigueur* on the part of the minister.

In the Highland church the practice of religion in the home was generally viewed as inseparable from that life of godliness which was proclaimed from the pulpit. Indeed it was commonly held that the spiritual vitality of the congregation could not rise above the level of godliness practised in the home. Hence the emphasis on family worship. Although the church disavowed the use of printed prayers in the pulpit, there was no shortage of devotional manuals including specimen prayers for use at family worship. Nevertheless, despite these aids to worship, it became increasingly difficult, even when the will was present, to sustain the habit of gathering the family for a formal act of worship either at the beginning or the end of the day. What had

9   Norman C Macfarlane, *Apostles of the North, Sketches of some Highland Ministers* (Stornoway, ND), p. 64.

been practical in a rural environment in which the daily routine was regulated by sunrise and sundown, became increasingly difficult in an urban environment governed by public transport timetables and radio and television schedules.

With the passing of the years the emphasis shifted from the family at worship — either in the home or in the church — to religious activities designed for different age-groups; and ministers, even those of conservative Highland congregations, found their energies to be increasingly absorbed by organisational rather than spiritual tasks. Separation between parents and children was further accentuated when they ceased to share a common language for the practice of religion. Curiously, long after Gaelic-speaking parents had abandoned the Gaelic language in the workplace and seldom had recourse to it in the home, they continued to show a preference for it at worship. It was for this reason that many Gaelic congregations delayed the introduction of English services with disastrous consequences for the spiritual welfare of the rising generation. But, if congregations were to survive, change had to come. Now Gaelic services are at best a fringe activity with Highland congregations in the cities. Despite the current educational emphasis on Gaelic as a spoken language it is doubtful if it can ever be reinstated as the common language of worship. As a vehicle of worship it must remain the province of the aficionados of the language — those who have had extensive exposure to Gaelic worship in its Highland or Island setting and who have come to understand and appreciate the nuances which it communicates. As such, even in the Hebrides, let alone in the cities, it can only cater for a minority interest.

Meantime what remains of traditional Highland presbyterian worship survives within the residue of Glasgow's erstwhile Gaelic congregations. Many factors doubtless will influence the perpetuation or demise of that tradition. At the present time the forms and styles of worship attaching to many different traditions are in the melting-pot. One-time innovations such as hymns and organs are now passé and outmoded. Formal worship in the context of a church building is likewise under suspicion in some quarters. Whether the Reformed tradition in its Highland setting can survive at a time when the church is disowning so much of its past, must be open to question. The continued use of the Metrical Psalter together with a familiar version of the Scriptures would seem to be the minimal requirements for the preservation of the tradition. Many today query the relevance of traditional versions and practices but a system that has raised worship based on the Authorised Version and the Scottish Metrical Psalter to the level of an art-form, may in this conservation-minded age, yet find its champions and defenders.